Positive Influence for Future Impact

Positive Influence for Future Impact

Dr. Nigel L Walker

WLI Unpublisher Services, LLC

Contents

Introduction   1

Chapter 1: The Positive Influence Mindset   3

Chapter 2: Leading with Vision, Not Position   8

Chapter 3: Cultivating Leadership at Every Level   17

Chapter 4: Purpose-Driven Planning   35

Chapter 5: The Power of Relationships   51

Chapter 6: Resilience and Recovery   69

Chapter 7: Vision, Voice, and Values   86

Chapter 8: Empathy in Action   103

Chapter 9: The Momentum of Integrity   120

Chapter 10: Intentional Growth and Learning   137

Chapter 11: Cultivating Community Impact   154

Chapter 12: Legacy Through Service   172

Chapter 13: A Call to Positive Action   188

Final Summary and Closing Takeaway   203

About the Author   206

Introduction

I wrote Positive Influence for Future Impact because I believe that positive influence is an essential attribute for anyone who occupies—or aspires to—a position of leadership. Leadership isn't always about titles or formal roles. Often, it's found in the way we show up for others—in our families, workplaces, classrooms, and communities. Whether assigned or assumed, leadership is ultimately about impact. And to lead well, to lead meaningfully, we must lead with influence that uplifts, inspires, and motivates others toward their highest potential.

Through my personal and professional journey as an educator and leader, I have come to recognize that influence is not passive. It is an intentional act. When we lead with purpose, integrity, compassion, and conviction, we begin to see transformation—not just in outcomes, but in people. Positive influence is the invisible thread that connects great leaders to great results. It empowers individuals to believe in themselves, to push beyond perceived limits, and to contribute to something greater than themselves.

This book is a reflection of that belief. It offers insights drawn from real experiences and practical lessons that speak to the heart of leadership—lessons about motivation, resilience, communication, and service. It encourages readers to consider not just how they lead, but why they lead, and what legacy they hope to leave behind. Each

1

page aims to spark self-reflection, ignite action, and help you grow into a leader who makes others better.

Whether you are a principal guiding a school, a manager building a team, a parent raising a family, or a community member seeking change, the principles in this book are meant for you. They are grounded in the idea that leadership is not about control, but about connection. Not about power, but about purpose. And not about being in charge, but about being of service.

By the time you finish this book, I hope you'll be reminded of the tremendous influence you hold—and inspired to use it with intention. You have the capacity to make a lasting difference in the lives of others. Positive Influence for Future Impact is both a reminder and a roadmap. Let it guide you as you lead with authenticity, compassion, and unwavering purpose.

Chapter 1: The Positive Influence Mindset

Influence is not about power; it's about presence. It's the quiet force behind every movement, the steady pulse beneath effective leadership, and the catalyst that sparks transformation in others. As a motivational speaker and an educational leader, I have witnessed how the right mindset can shape outcomes far beyond one's immediate reach. The positive influence mindset starts with self-awareness.

You cannot lead others until you've first confronted and led yourself. This means embracing your values, owning your story, and recognizing the impact your behavior has on those around you. Influence is not a switch you flip when convenient—it is a lifestyle of intentional action, service, and reflection. In schools, boardrooms, and community centers, I've seen firsthand how those who understand their influence can shift culture. They listen differently.

They speak with purpose. They inspire hope in those who have forgotten how to hope. The positive influence mindset says, 'I don't need a title to make a difference. I just need to show up with integrity and courage.' One of the most powerful realizations a leader can have is that influence multiplies.

When we model resilience, others reflect it. When we extend grace, others grow into it. When we uplift voices, we amplify change.

The positive influence mindset doesn't just elevate individuals—it empowers communities. To develop a positive influence mindset, one must cultivate consistency.

Inconsistency breeds mistrust, while daily dependability builds confidence. Whether you're leading a team or raising a family, the moments that shape lives are often small, quiet, and unseen. Influence isn't about grand gestures—it's about the habits that reveal our character day by day. To embrace a positive influence mindset is to understand that our greatest power often lies in the smallest decisions. Influence doesn't announce itself; it unfolds through consistency, character, and compassion.

It begins when we choose to be present in our own growth so we can be present for the growth of others. As a former principal, I learned quickly that the power of influence is less about directives and more about modeling. A hallway greeting, a note of encouragement, a pause to listen—these small acts were sometimes more impactful than any formal policy or program. Influence is rarely dramatic. It is often subtle, organic, and personal.

Every leader must wrestle with the truth that influence begins at the intersection of trust and humility. Titles may open doors, but only character keeps them open. When I was first placed in charge of a struggling academic team, I had to earn the respect of the staff not by demanding compliance but by modeling commitment. In educational settings, the positive influence mindset transforms classrooms into launchpads. A teacher who believes in the potential of a student, even when that student cannot yet see it, becomes a powerful force in that child's trajectory.

This belief must be intentional, rooted in both high expectations and deep empathy. Beyond education, influence shows up in our homes, in our places of worship, and in our community efforts. The father who leads by example, the pastor who uplifts without judgment, the volunteer who consistently shows up—these are influencers who rarely trend on social media but shape lives for generations. Influence is also tied to resilience. When challenges come—and they will—the person with a positive influence mindset doesn't retreat.

Instead, they reflect, adjust, and press forward. This steady persistence teaches others that leadership is not about being perfect; it's about being anchored in purpose. A crucial aspect of developing the positive influence mindset is emotional regulation. Leaders who cannot manage their own emotions will struggle to manage teams, classrooms, or communities. When we are emotionally grounded, we create safe and empowering environments where others can thrive.

I've spoken with countless leaders who initially believed influence meant speaking louder or exerting more control. Over time, they discovered that it meant listening more deeply, guiding with clarity, and demonstrating unwavering integrity. Real influence is often quiet but deeply felt. Finally, cultivating the positive influence mindset requires ongoing self-reflection. Who are you when the crowd is gone?

What principles anchor your decisions? When you lead with influence, your presence becomes a source of peace, motivation, and vision. That is how futures are shaped—one choice, one life, one influence at a time. The positive influence mindset is not born from perfection, but from authenticity. People are drawn to leaders who are real—those who acknowledge mistakes, own their weaknesses, and are transparent about their growth journey.

Authenticity builds bridges where authority can sometimes create barriers. When people see that you are relatable, they are more likely to follow your lead, trust your vision, and believe in their own ability to lead. As a principal, I learned that influence is more sustainable than control. When you influence someone, they change because they want to—not because they have to. I saw this in students who transformed their behavior not because of consequences, but because they felt seen, valued, and respected.

When they believed I had their best interest at heart, they were more open to correction, more willing to grow. Influence also requires emotional intelligence. A leader must be attuned not only to their own emotions but also to the emotional climate of their environment. The ability to read the room, to sense when a conversation needs empathy over efficiency, is a skill that separates transactional managers from transformational leaders. It's the difference between pushing for outcomes and inspiring commitment.

In community leadership, I've come to understand that influence expands when it's shared. Too often, leaders hoard power, believing their light will dim if others shine. But real influence multiplies. When you elevate others, you create a culture where leadership is distributed and everyone feels empowered to contribute. Influence becomes contagious.

Your influence is not limited by your position; it's amplified by your posture. A posture of humility invites collaboration. A posture of curiosity fosters innovation. A posture of service builds loyalty. In every setting—whether addressing a staff meeting or mentoring a student—how you carry yourself communicates volumes about what you value and who you are.

Storytelling is one of the most powerful tools of influence. I've found that sharing personal stories of struggle, growth, and resilience allows others to see themselves in your journey. It breaks down the illusion of distance and hierarchy. It says, 'I've been where you are.' And that connection becomes the foundation for influence that's grounded in empathy. A key lesson in my speaking career has been this: influence is rooted in value.

If people don't believe you add value to their lives, they will not follow you. That's why preparation, insight, and sincerity are nonnegotiables. Every stage, every mic, every opportunity to speak is a chance to deliver something that uplifts, informs, or transforms. Leaders with a positive influence mindset invest in relationships long before they need results. Influence is earned in the spaces between transactions—in the hallway conversations, the check-in texts, the moments when you show up not because it's required, but because it's right.

These moments build relational capital, and that capital becomes influence. In personal life, the positive influence mindset can revolutionize parenting. Children are not moved by lectures as much as they are shaped by what they observe. A parent who models integrity, discipline, and compassion teaches volumes without saying a word. The same is true in marriage, friendships, and mentorship—our actions preach louder than our intentions.

One overlooked element of influence is consistency in character. A leader who shifts values based on the audience will never inspire long-term trust. Influence requires alignment—between what we say and how we live. Between what we promote and what we practice. Integrity is the invisible thread that weaves trust into influence.

Self-care is also a component of influence often neglected. A burnt-out leader cannot pour into others. Influence requires emotional stamina, mental clarity, and physical vitality. When we neglect our well-being, our capacity to lead diminishes. That's why rest, reflection, and renewal are not luxuries—they are leadership essentials.

In all this, influence is not a destination but a discipline. It is cultivated in daily choices, refined in challenges, and sustained by a sense of calling. Whether you're leading a classroom, an organization, a household, or a movement, the positive influence mindset transforms not only those around you—but you, as well. As we close this chapter, let me leave you with a final thought: Influence is not granted by status; it is earned through service. The most influential leaders I've known weren't loud—they were consistent.

They didn't chase applause—they chased impact. They didn't force change—they modeled it until others chose it. That is the true power of influence.

Chapter 2: Leading with Vision, Not Position

True leadership isn't defined by title or hierarchy—it's defined by vision. A leader's position may grant them authority, but it is their vision that inspires trust, motivates action, and fuels transformation. Visionary leaders see beyond what is to what could be, and that capacity to imagine, articulate, and build a better future is what sets them apart.

When I reflect on my time as a principal, I can remember moments when the job description alone would not have carried me through. The bureaucratic responsibilities, the endless meetings, and the unexpected crises were always present—but what kept me grounded was the vision I held for the students, teachers, and the culture we were building. That vision gave meaning to the chaos. Visionary leadership requires courage. It takes courage to challenge the status quo, to speak truth in a room full of silence, to advocate for the unseen and unheard.

Leadership that relies only on position will always play it safe. But leadership guided by vision will press forward even when it's uncomfortable, uncertain, or unpopular. Leaders who lead with vision operate with clarity and purpose. They communicate not just where they are going, but why it matters. People follow clarity, not confusion.

They are drawn to leaders who can paint a picture of the future that's worth working toward. When people can see themselves in the vision, they take ownership of the mission. One of the most vital responsibilities of a visionary leader is to cultivate belief. Vision without belief is fantasy. Vision with belief becomes a movement.

I remember standing in front of staff during professional development, not just outlining goals, but describing the possibilities. I shared stories, asked for input, and linked our daily routines to the outcomes we all cared about. That process created alignment—and with alignment came momentum. In education and beyond, leading with vision means becoming a storyteller of possibility. Facts inform, but stories transform.

When leaders tell stories that humanize the work, that connect head to heart, they begin to mobilize people on a deeper level. Stories have the power to carry vision across barriers of skepticism and fatigue. Visionary leadership is also anchored in values. Vision without values can become manipulation. It's not enough to have a dream; it must be rooted in integrity.

People must trust that the vision is not a tool for personal gain, but a vehicle for collective progress. That trust is built in how leaders show up—consistently, transparently, and ethically. A leader's vision is also tested in adversity. When setbacks come—and they always do—people look to the leader for direction. This is where vision becomes a stabilizer.

A clear and compelling vision gives people a reason to persist through obstacles. It turns problems into puzzles, delays into detours, and crises into catalysts for growth. Great leaders don't keep their vision to themselves. They communicate it repeatedly, creatively, and passionately. They embed it in meetings, messages, and moments of recognition.

They ensure that everyone—no matter their role—can articulate the vision in their own words. When vision becomes part of the culture, it shapes decisions, fuels resilience, and fosters unity. As a motivational speaker, I often tell audiences: You don't need permission to lead. You need a purpose. Position is temporary, but vision is transferable.

Anyone—regardless of their job title—can lead if they are clear about what they stand for and bold enough to act on it. This kind of leadership creates ripple effects in organizations, communities, and families. Visionary leadership is not a destination; it is a discipline. It requires the leader to step back often, reflect, recalibrate, and recommit. It asks us to keep our eyes on what matters most, even when the immediate demands try to pull us off course.

When we lead with vision, we help others rise above the noise and focus on what's truly possible. One of the clearest indicators of visionary leadership is a relentless focus on growth. Visionary leaders don't settle for maintaining systems—they continuously search for ways to elevate them. Whether it's improving instruction in schools, streamlining operations in business, or building unity in a fractured community, these leaders always ask, 'How can we do better?' They don't just see potential—they pursue it with intensity. I remember working with a team of teachers who were burned out, cynical, and resistant to change.

They had seen too many initiatives come and go. What shifted things wasn't another mandate—it was a renewed sense of purpose. We stopped talking about compliance and started talking about impact. We revisited our 'why.' Once they could see how their daily work connected to something bigger than a test score, momentum returned. Visionary leaders know how to personalize the mission.

It's not enough to cast a broad, sweeping vision. The best leaders help individuals see how they fit into that vision. This means listening deeply, understanding strengths, and speaking in language that resonates. It means acknowledging the humanity of the people you lead. When people feel personally invested, they give more than effort—they give heart.

Another mark of visionary leadership is flexibility. While vision must be steadfast, the path to achieving it must be adaptable. Circumstances change, and a wise leader knows how to adjust tactics without abandoning core principles. The pandemic taught all of us that agility is not optional. Leaders who clung to rigid plans were outpaced by those who could pivot while keeping their vision intact.

Vision also thrives on collaboration. A leader with vision invites others into the process—not to rubber-stamp ideas, but to co-create solutions. Collaboration turns vision from a personal dream into a shared mission. It increases buy-in and surfaces perspectives that improve decision-making. I often say, 'If your vision can't fit more voices, it's not big enough.'

In community leadership, the power of vision is seen most clearly when people begin to believe that change is possible. I've led neighborhood initiatives where the first hurdle wasn't funding or logistics—it was hopelessness. Visionary leadership begins by helping people imagine something better. Once that hope is kindled, strategy and support can follow. A visionary leader must also be a systems thinker.

Big dreams falter when they're not grounded in structure. The leader must connect vision to strategy and systems. That means developing processes, creating feedback loops, and aligning resources to support the dream. It's not just about inspiration—it's about implementation. Integrity is the bedrock of visionary leadership.

People need to trust not just the dream, but the dreamer. That trust is built day by day, decision by decision. It's in how you treat people, how you admit mistakes, and how consistently you act on your values. When your character is clear, your vision becomes more compelling. Visionary leadership leaves a legacy.

It doesn't just solve today's problems; it sets the stage for future progress. The schools we build, the businesses we grow, the communities we empower—these become the footprints of vision made real. They outlast us. And that's the point. The ultimate goal of leading with vision is not recognition, but generational impact.

As you reflect on your own leadership, ask yourself: Am I leading with vision or just reacting to demands? Am I shaping the future or merely surviving the present? Real influence is found in those who dare to dream, plan, and lead with intention. Vision is not about grandeur—it's about direction. And the clearer your direction, the stronger your influence becomes.

Leadership rooted in vision transcends day-to-day responsibilities. It lifts people from the realm of duty into the realm of destiny. A janitor cleaning a hallway with a sense of purpose, knowing he's creating a safe environment for learning, is living proof that vision can dignify every task. That's the power of a visionary leader—to make the ordinary extraordinary through perspective. One of the core responsibilities of a visionary leader is to remain forward-thinking.

They anticipate needs before crises emerge and prepare others for what's ahead. In education, this might mean introducing innovative instructional models before standardized test scores decline. In business, it could involve digital transformation before competitors gain a foothold. In communities, it might mean investing in youth leadership before apathy takes root. Vision isn't just seeing the future—it's preparing for it.

Visionary leaders must also learn to communicate vision with passion and clarity across different platforms and to varied audiences. It's one thing to articulate a compelling mission to a board of directors; it's another to inspire a group of teenagers in an after-school program. Each group requires a unique message crafted with care and rooted in the same overarching purpose. This ability to translate vision across levels is what drives momentum. Momentum is not self-sustaining.

Even a strong vision can lose energy over time if not nurtured and protected. Visionary leaders understand the importance of rhythm—of setting short-term wins to celebrate progress. They identify milestones, create celebrations, and help their teams recognize growth. These checkpoints sustain belief during tough seasons. They remind people, 'We are moving forward.

We are not stuck.' Many times, visionaries must also protect their teams from distraction. Not every opportunity aligns with the core mission. The temptation to chase trends or respond to pressure can pull leaders off course. A visionary leader has the courage to say no—not out of fear, but out of focus.

They discern what fits and what doesn't. They make decisions not for applause but for alignment. Resilience is another defining trait of visionary leaders. Anyone can cast a vision when circumstances are favorable. But it takes grit and grace to continue painting the picture of a better future when reality is full of setbacks, resistance, and limited resources.

In those moments, leaders are tested not on their eloquence, but on their endurance. When the leader stays steady, others find hope. A transformational aspect of visionary leadership is the cultivation of legacy. Visionary leaders are not consumed by their own success—they are obsessed with generational impact. They mentor successors, document their learning, and embed values into systems that will outlast them.

They know that real leadership isn't about being indispensable—it's about making others capable. This legacy mindset changes how decisions are made. Instead of focusing on what's easiest or most popular, visionary leaders ask, 'What will matter ten years from now?' They invest in character, community partnerships, and sustainable infrastructure. Whether in education or business, they build for longevity, not likes. Their influence grows because it is not centered on self.

Technology plays a growing role in visionary leadership. Leaders must use tools not just to automate tasks but to amplify mission. Social media, data analytics, learning platforms—all can be leveraged to communicate, track, and accelerate vision. But these tools must remain subordinate to purpose. When technology serves the mission, it becomes a multiplier.

When it replaces vision, it becomes a distraction. An often-overlooked element of visionary leadership is rest. Visionaries must protect time to think, reflect, and renew. Constant busyness can cloud vision. The leader who never pauses eventually loses perspective.

Vision grows in quiet spaces—in the margins of the calendar. Rest is not a sign of weakness; it's a discipline of clarity. Another critical aspect of visionary leadership is the modeling of behavior. People listen to what leaders say, but they follow what leaders do. A visionary who speaks of innovation but clings to outdated practices creates confusion.

A visionary who preaches collaboration but hoards power breeds resentment. Alignment between message and model creates credibility, and credibility sustains vision. In every field, from education to corporate leadership, the same principle applies: your vision must outgrow you. It must inspire others to dream, lead, and contribute in ways that evolve beyond your influence. This is the ultimate measure of success—not how many people followed your plan, but how many were empowered to shape their own.

I have seen firsthand how visionary leadership can transform schools, uplift families, and inspire entire communities. But I've also seen how quickly influence fades when vision is absent. People disengage. Energy drains. Conflict increases.

Without vision, leadership becomes maintenance. With vision, leadership becomes movement. In closing this chapter, I leave you with a challenge: Don't wait for position to give you permission. Lead with vision. Let your passion clarify your path.

Let your integrity guide your actions. And let your presence—fueled by purpose—spark change that outlasts you. That is the power of vision, and that is the call of true leadership. Visionary leaders are also effective mentors. They recognize that part of their role is to develop future leaders, not just manage current followers.

Mentorship becomes a natural extension of vision because it ensures continuity. When leaders take time to invest in others—through coaching, encouragement, and challenging assignments—they extend the reach of their vision beyond their own presence. Creating space for others to lead is not a threat to visionary leadership—it is the fulfillment of it. The greatest visions require collaboration across multiple levels of an organization or community. Visionary leaders do not fear the rise of others.

They foster it. They believe that when others succeed, the mission advances. That shift in mindset—from personal achievement to collective elevation—is what defines lasting impact. Cultural awareness is another layer that visionary leaders must develop. A vision that inspires one group may fall flat with another if it's not contextualized appropriately.

Effective leaders are learners of people. They immerse themselves in the languages, values, and lived experiences of those they hope to lead. They adapt their communication and goals to reflect the diversity within their reach without diluting their core message. Visionary leadership also demands ethical courage. There will be moments when doing what's right conflicts with what's easy.

In those moments, the clarity of the vision becomes a moral compass. Whether advocating for equity in schools or standing up to unjust business practices, visionary leaders choose what's principled over what's profitable. Their conviction breeds credibility. Celebrating progress is an underrated but essential habit for sustaining vision. The journey toward a bold future can be exhausting.

People need to know that their efforts are seen and that their sacrifices matter. Visionary leaders find ways to honor the steps along the way. Whether through public recognition, reflective meetings, or personal notes of appreciation, they weave celebration into the culture. Another hallmark of visionary leadership is its ability to simplify complexity. Vision brings clarity to chaos.

It helps teams prioritize what matters most. A leader with vision doesn't react to every urgency—they respond to what aligns with long-term goals. They guide people through noise and distraction by continually pointing back to purpose. This clarity reduces burnout and enhances effectiveness. In my experience leading community-based initiatives, I've learned that visionary leaders must be storytellers, strategists, and stewards—all at once.

They must tell a compelling story of what could be. They must build a strategy to make it happen. And they must steward the people, time, and resources entrusted to them with excellence. Balancing those roles is not easy, but it is essential. Vision is sustained not just through planning, but through reflection.

Great leaders take time to revisit their original purpose. They ask: Are we drifting? Are we growing? Are we still aligned? This reflection protects the vision from becoming obsolete or corrupted by ego.

It keeps the mission pure and the path purposeful. Finally, visionary leaders operate with a sense of urgency—not panic, but purpose. They understand that windows of opportunity don't stay open forever. They act decisively when timing demands it. They don't wait for permission to lead change—they recognize the responsibility of their position and the power of their voice.

That urgency, when rooted in clarity and compassion, inspires action. Leadership without vision is management at best. But leadership with vision is transformation. It lifts people out of the ordinary into the realm of purpose. It creates cultures of excellence, movements of meaning, and legacies that echo for generations. Chapter 2 reminds us that you don't need a title to be a leader—but if you carry a vision, you carry influence. And that influence can shape the world.

Chapter 3: Cultivating Leadership at Every Level

Leadership is not confined to corner offices or executive titles—it is a capacity that exists within everyone, waiting to be cultivated. The notion that only a select few are 'born to lead' is outdated and limiting.

Leadership today must be seen as a shared responsibility, nurtured at every level of an organization or community. When individuals are empowered to lead from where they are, the potential for growth and innovation multiplies exponentially. Cultivating leadership at every level begins with a cultural shift. It means creating an environment where initiative is encouraged, voices are heard, and contributions are valued regardless of position. This culture does not arise by accident; it must be intentionally designed by senior leaders who model trust, collaboration, and growth.

They must shift from controlling outcomes to developing people—a fundamental transition from command-and-control to coach-and-cultivate. I've seen firsthand how transformational it can be when organizations empower teachers to lead beyond their classrooms, students to lead among peers, and custodians to lead through excellence in service. Leadership becomes less about hierarchy and more about influence. It becomes embedded in the fabric of the culture, where everyone takes ownership for excellence, not because they are told to—but because they are inspired to. This type of leadership is developmental.

It requires systems that identify potential, offer skill-building, and provide stretch opportunities. Professional development should not only be reserved for those with management roles. Workshops on emotional intelligence, public speaking, problem-solving, and strategic thinking should be offered widely. Mentorship programs, peer coaching, and cross-functional teams provide fertile ground for growth. One of the most effective tools for cultivating leadership is feedback.

Constructive, ongoing feedback helps people reflect, adjust, and grow. In organizations that thrive, feedback is not feared—it is welcomed as fuel for development. Leaders must not only give feedback but also model receiving it. When team members see leaders responding to feedback with humility and action, it sets the tone for a learning culture. Trust is the currency of distributed leadership.

Empowering others to lead requires a willingness to release control. This does not mean abdicating responsibility—it means believing in others and providing them with the autonomy to innovate. Micromanagement suffocates leadership. Trust liberates it. Leaders who delegate effectively and affirm the decisions of others cultivate confidence and creativity.

Leadership development must be embedded in daily practice, not isolated in special programs. Team meetings should include leadership challenges and learning moments. Projects should rotate leadership roles to give different individuals the chance to guide. Reflection should be built into workflows, helping individuals assess how they are showing up and where they are growing. When leadership is seen as a daily discipline rather than an occasional title, everyone begins to engage differently.

In community settings, cultivating leadership means identifying and nurturing local champions. These may be parents, business owners, clergy, or young people with a spark of vision. Community leadership is not about waiting for saviors—it's about equipping citizens. Training programs, leadership circles, and civic engagement opportunities create pipelines of influence where people feel equipped and inspired to lead change in their neighborhoods. Schools are one of the most fertile grounds for cultivating leadership at every level.

From student councils to classroom jobs, from peer mentoring to schoolwide initiatives, students can learn that leadership is about service, initiative, and responsibility. When students are trusted to lead, they develop agency, accountability, and confidence. The same holds true for teachers. Instructional leadership, committee work, and innovation grants can turn a teacher into a changemaker within their own building. Ultimately, cultivating leadership at every level creates resilience.

When leadership is shared, the organization or community does not collapse when one leader departs. Continuity is built into the system. Innovation comes from every direction. And people feel a deep sense of belonging and purpose. Leadership becomes not just a role—but a way of being.

That is the kind of culture that endures. Leadership begins with self-awareness. In order to cultivate leadership at every level, individuals must be encouraged to reflect on their strengths, weaknesses, values, and goals. Self-aware individuals are better equipped to lead authentically and align their actions with their principles. Reflection exercises, self-assessments, and coaching sessions are powerful tools to deepen this awareness and inspire personal growth.

Confidence is a product of competence and encouragement. Organizations that want to cultivate leadership must ensure that individuals feel supported as they take on new challenges. This includes not only training and skill development but also positive reinforcement. When people are affirmed for their contributions, they become more willing to step into leadership roles. Confidence builds the courage to speak up, take initiative, and persist through adversity.

Emotional intelligence is a cornerstone of effective leadership. Leaders at every level must learn to manage their own emotions and respond effectively to the emotions of others. Cultivating emotional intelligence means teaching empathy, active listening, and conflict resolution. It also means modeling calm and clarity in stressful moments. Emotionally intelligent leaders build stronger relationships and more resilient teams.

Shared leadership structures promote empowerment and accountability. By creating collaborative leadership models—like teacher-led teams, peer-led workgroups, or resident advisory boards—organizations distribute influence and responsibility. This not only increases engagement but also fosters innovation, as more voices contribute to decision-making. Shared leadership does not dilute authority; it amplifies effectiveness. One essential ingredient in leadership development is storytelling.

When individuals hear real examples of peers stepping into leadership roles and creating change, they are inspired to see themselves as capable of doing the same. Storytelling also serves as a cultural mirror, reinforcing the values and behaviors that define effective leadership in that organization or community. Inclusion must be intentional. Leadership cultivation should not be reserved for a select few who fit a traditional mold. Equity in leadership development means proactively seeking out individuals who may have been overlooked—whether due to race, gender, socio-economic background, or other factors—and inviting them into growth opportunities.

Inclusive leadership models are not only more just; they are also more dynamic and effective. Feedback loops should be part of the leadership culture. In addition to receiving feedback, aspiring leaders should be trained to give it—constructively and compassionately. Creating environments where feedback is frequent, normalized, and aligned to vision strengthens the organization's overall leadership capacity. When people are taught how to have hard conversations with empathy and clarity, they grow into leaders others trust.

Leadership opportunities should begin early. In schools, this means creating meaningful roles for students as young as elementary age to contribute to school culture. In organizations, this might involve internships, early-career leadership tracks, or reverse mentoring programs. By starting early, we instill the belief that leadership is not something you wait for—it's something you practice every day. Failure should be reframed as part of the leadership journey.

One of the most damaging mindsets is the fear of making mistakes. Leaders must model learning from failure and celebrate effort, reflection, and resilience. Post-project reviews, journaling exercises, and storytelling sessions about past failures can help normalize struggle as a stepping stone to success. Vision must be local and personal. While strategic goals may be defined at the top, leaders at every level should be invited to develop a sense of purpose within their sphere of influence.

This ensures that everyone has a personal stake in the vision and is motivated to contribute to its realization. Leaders who connect their daily work to a larger mission are more inspired, focused, and impactful. Communities thrive when leadership is cultivated across age groups. Seniors bring wisdom and lived experience; youth bring energy and creativity. When intergenerational leadership models are adopted, both groups learn from one another, bridging gaps and building mutual respect.

Programs that pair youth leaders with community elders, for example, can create powerful mentorship and cultural continuity. Leadership is sustained by community. The most resilient leaders are those who feel connected and supported by a network of peers. Cultivating leadership means fostering relationships where leaders can share challenges, exchange ideas, and celebrate wins together. Peer networks, learning communities, and mastermind groups are powerful vehicles for sustaining leadership over time.

Resilient leadership cultures prioritize wellness. Burnout is the enemy of leadership sustainability. Organizations must promote mental health, work-life balance, and restorative practices. Leaders should be encouraged to set boundaries, take breaks, and model balance for those they lead. A leader who is whole is better equipped to support and inspire others.

In educational spaces, teachers should be seen as leaders of learning—not just deliverers of content. Instructional leadership includes using data to inform practice, mentoring colleagues, and innovating in the classroom. When teachers are given autonomy and recognition as thought leaders, school culture transforms. Empowered educators create empowered students. Authenticity is the currency of leadership in today's world.

People want to follow leaders who are real—who own their stories, admit their flaws, and stay grounded in values. Developing authentic leaders means creating space for vulnerability, reflection, and identity exploration. Leadership programs should not only focus on skills but on the cultivation of self. To build leadership at every level, organizations must embed leadership into evaluations and goal-setting. This helps individuals prioritize leadership behaviors in their own growth plans.

Whether through leadership competencies, peer evaluations, or 360-feedback systems, integrating leadership into performance conversations helps reinforce its value. Technology can be a tool for cultivating leadership, especially in distributed or hybrid teams. Virtual leadership training, digital collaboration platforms, and online mentoring systems make it possible to scale leadership development. However, technology should never replace human connection—it should support it. Leaders must be taught how to leverage digital tools without losing personal engagement.

Leadership must be measured by more than productivity. Metrics like engagement, innovation, collaboration, and growth mindsets should be part of how leadership impact is assessed. Data dashboards, storytelling evaluations, and qualitative surveys all offer insights into how well leadership is being developed and practiced across the organization. In environments where leadership is cultivated at every level, everyone sees themselves as a contributor to the culture. There is less blame, more initiative.

Less fear, more creativity. Less waiting, more doing. A leadership-rich culture is one where people take ownership not just of tasks—but of the collective vision. It's a space where people bring their full selves to the table and are celebrated for it. Ultimately, the goal of cultivating leadership at every level is not just organizational success—it is human flourishing.

When people are trusted, empowered, and supported, they grow not only in competence but in confidence and character. They become more than employees or members—they become change agents, culture carriers, and leaders for life. One of the most effective ways to embed leadership into a culture is by decentralizing decision-making. When decisions are made closer to the point of action, people feel more invested in outcomes. This cultivates ownership and fosters accountability.

Empowering people to make decisions within their roles—guided by clear principles and shared vision—unlocks creativity and reduces dependency on upper management. Leadership also grows through cross-functional collaboration. When individuals from different departments, grade levels, or disciplines come together to solve problems, they gain exposure to new ideas and develop broader leadership perspectives. These collaborations break down silos and teach participants to lead with empathy, humility, and an appreciation for complexity. Creating pathways for leadership advancement is crucial.

People must see a future in their organization that includes them in influential roles. This includes vertical mobility—such as becoming a team lead or supervisor—but also horizontal growth, like leading new initiatives or mentoring others. Leadership development must be seen as fluid and multidimensional. Transparency is an underrated leadership trait that organizations should intentionally foster. Leaders at all levels need to learn how to communicate clearly and openly about challenges, successes, and rationale for decisions.

When transparency becomes the norm, trust grows, and emerging leaders feel safe stepping into responsibility without fear of hidden agendas. Another important aspect of cultivating leadership is encouraging people to lead according to their strengths. Not every leader will be charismatic or outspoken. Some lead through listening, others through organizing, others through creative problem-solving. By helping individuals identify and maximize their unique leadership style, organizations cultivate a diversity of approaches that strengthen the whole.

Recognition plays a vital role in leadership development. When people are acknowledged for their contributions—especially when stepping out of their comfort zone—they are more likely to continue taking initiative. Recognition can be public or private, formal or informal, but it must be sincere and specific. Celebrating leadership behaviors reinforces them. Leadership thrives when people are encouraged to innovate.

Cultivating a culture where experimentation is welcome—and failure is seen as a step toward success—unleashes energy and imagination. Leaders should be taught how to run pilot programs, gather feedback, adjust strategies, and reflect on outcomes. This iterative process is at the heart of both leadership and learning. Organizations that want to develop leaders must also be willing to have hard conversations. Feedback about performance, alignment, or interpersonal dynamics must be timely and courageous.

Training emerging leaders to navigate difficult conversations with clarity and compassion builds maturity and emotional resilience. Reflection is a foundational leadership practice. Leaders should be encouraged to journal, meditate, or engage in regular debriefs. This not only sharpens self-awareness but deepens insight into team dynamics, organizational goals, and personal calling. Reflective leaders are more adaptive and grounded in purpose.

Purpose is what sustains leaders over time. Cultivating leadership at every level means helping individuals connect their personal mission to the mission of the organization or cause. When people understand why their work matters, they engage with deeper motivation. This sense of purpose becomes a wellspring of energy and persistence. Resilience in leadership doesn't just emerge in crises—it's built in everyday moments of perseverance.

When leaders are taught to face setbacks with a growth mindset, to regulate their emotions, and to lean on support networks, they develop staying power. Cultivating resilience must be an intentional part of leadership programs. Mentorship is one of the most powerful tools for developing leaders. Pairing emerging leaders with experienced mentors accelerates growth and builds intergenerational learning. These relationships also reduce isolation and create a sense of belonging.

Mentorship should be reciprocal, with mentors also gaining fresh insights from mentees. Organizations should conduct regular leadership audits. These reviews examine who holds formal and informal influence, how leadership opportunities are distributed, and where gaps exist. Leadership audits help ensure equity, identify emerging talent, and uncover systemic barriers to participation. Creating a shared language around leadership enhances consistency.

When everyone in an organization understands what leadership looks like, sounds like, and feels like, they can support each other's development. Core leadership competencies, values-based frameworks, and behavioral rubrics all support a common understanding of leadership expectations. Spirituality and moral grounding can be essential components of leadership development, particularly in values-driven organizations. Exploring questions of ethics, service, legacy, and responsibility can strengthen character and deepen a leader's commitment to others. When leaders are rooted in something greater than themselves, their influence becomes transformative.

Storytelling continues to be one of the most effective leadership tools. Leaders must learn to tell stories that convey vision, celebrate growth, and honor the journey. Storytelling helps humanize leadership and make abstract goals relatable. Training in storytelling should be part of any leadership curriculum. Peer leadership opportunities are especially valuable in group environments.

Rotating leadership among peers in teams, clubs, or committees gives everyone a chance to build and flex their skills. These experiences also build empathy, as leaders learn what it feels like to guide others—and to be guided. Leading through service is one of the most impactful leadership models. When individuals lead by prioritizing the well-being and development of others, they build loyalty and drive cultural change. Service leadership emphasizes listening, empathy, and empowerment—qualities that strengthen communities and organizations alike.

Leadership succession planning is a critical but often neglected component of leadership cultivation. Developing a clear plan for who will take over key roles ensures continuity and reduces instability during transitions. Succession planning also signals to emerging leaders that there is a future pathway for them. Finally, leadership at every level must be embedded in the organization's identity. It must be part of how people think, act, and relate to one another.

This means aligning policies, practices, rewards, and rituals around leadership values. When leadership becomes a way of life—not just a program—organizations and communities thrive. Leadership at every level thrives when individuals are given opportunities to engage in strategic thinking. This means more than just task execution—it involves encouraging people to anticipate challenges, evaluate options, and make informed decisions that align with long-term goals. Strategic thinking should be a taught skill, not assumed.

Through scenario planning, project-based challenges, and reflective dialogues, team members at all levels can develop the foresight and critical analysis needed to make visionary contributions. Another essential element of cultivating widespread leadership is the use of collaborative problem-solving frameworks. When teams work through structured models like design thinking or SWOT analysis, they learn how to approach issues from multiple angles. These tools teach leaders to listen first, define problems clearly, and test solutions iteratively. The process becomes a shared learning experience that sharpens everyone's leadership acumen, regardless of their formal title.

Leadership often emerges in crisis. Therefore, cultivating leadership at every level includes preparing individuals to lead in moments of uncertainty. This requires training in resilience, decision-making under pressure, and adaptive thinking. Role-play scenarios, emergency response simulations, and crisis communication drills are excellent platforms for helping emerging leaders build the confidence and skills necessary to perform when the stakes are high. A critical piece of leadership cultivation is teaching leaders how to influence without authority.

Many leadership opportunities come before a person holds a formal title. In these cases, influence is built through trust, credibility, and consistent delivery. Teaching team members how to manage up, facilitate peer collaboration, and build coalitions gives them the tools to lead from any seat at the table. Leaders at all levels must also understand systems thinking—the ability to see how different parts of an organization or community interact and influence one another. When people understand interdependencies, they make better decisions and collaborate more effectively.

Systems thinking training should be embedded into leadership development curricula, allowing participants to grasp the broader context of their decisions and understand the ripple effects of their actions. Diversity of thought is a hallmark of a healthy leadership culture. When leadership is cultivated across identities, departments, and life experiences, it generates more inclusive innovation. Organizations should build leadership pipelines that reflect the communities they serve. Diverse teams make better decisions, address a wider array of needs, and model equity in action.

Personal storytelling plays a unique role in leadership growth. Leaders who reflect on and share their own journey create powerful emotional connections. These narratives inspire others, humanize leadership, and help build psychological safety. Teaching storytelling as a leadership skill equips individuals to communicate vision, build trust, and rally support in authentic ways. Another critical skill in leadership development is time management.

Leaders at every level are often balancing operational duties with vision-setting. Helping leaders identify their high-impact activities, delegate appropriately, and create space for strategic work increases their overall effectiveness. Time audits, accountability partners, and calendar planning workshops can all contribute to stronger time leadership. To sustain a culture of leadership, organizations must celebrate initiative. This means highlighting not only outcomes but also the courage to start.

When people see that new ideas and calculated risks are respected—even when they don't immediately succeed—they are more likely to experiment and innovate. Recognition programs and storytelling forums are great vehicles for showcasing and reinforcing these behaviors. Leaders should also be taught the value of curiosity. Questions drive improvement. Curiosity fuels learning, and learning drives innovation.

When organizations normalize asking questions, seeking feedback, and admitting what they don't know, they create an environment where leadership is grounded in growth, not perfection. The most effective leadership cultures are supported by intentional rituals. These rituals might include weekly leadership circles, monthly recognition ceremonies, or quarterly vision-setting retreats. Rituals provide structure and meaning to the leadership journey. They reinforce shared values, create moments of reflection, and provide space for renewal.

Digital leadership is now a vital competency for leaders at every level. With the rise of remote and hybrid work, leaders must learn how to communicate, motivate, and monitor progress in digital environments. This includes virtual meeting facilitation, asynchronous communication, and digital wellness. Training in these areas ensures that leaders are not only technologically capable but also human-centered in their approach. To truly embed leadership at every level, learning must be continuous.

Leadership development should not be a one-time event or a linear path. It must be an evolving process, fueled by feedback, enriched by experience, and supported by mentors. Continuous learning platforms, personal development plans, and on-demand resources can help leaders evolve at their own pace while aligning with organizational goals. Leaders must also learn the art of delegation—not as a way to offload work, but as a tool for development. When leaders delegate stretch assignments thoughtfully, they create learning opportunities for others and free up time to focus on strategic leadership.

Effective delegation is clear, respectful, and paired with coaching. It builds confidence in both the delegator and the receiver. Lastly, cultivating leadership at every level requires belief. Belief that everyone has leadership potential. Belief that leadership can be learned.

Belief that when individuals are trusted and supported, they rise to the occasion. This belief must be demonstrated daily through inclusive practices, consistent encouragement, and courageous investment. It is this belief that transforms workplaces, classrooms, and communities into ecosystems of leadership. Leadership at every level begins with mindset. The belief that leadership is not confined to titles, but is a practice accessible to all, must be embedded into the culture of any organization or community.

When individuals are encouraged to see themselves as leaders—regardless of their job descriptions or backgrounds—they begin to take ownership, act with purpose, and influence positive change. This shift in mindset is foundational to cultivating distributed leadership and ensures that no single person or position holds the monopoly on progress. At the heart of cultivating leadership is the recognition of individual potential. People often rise to the level of expectation placed upon them. When emerging leaders are identified and affirmed early, they are more likely to develop the confidence, skills, and initiative needed to lead.

This requires leaders to act as talent scouts, constantly seeking opportunities to recognize contributions, build capacity, and create pathways for others to grow. A culture that sees leadership potential in everyone ensures a deep bench of talent and sustains long-term success. Shared leadership models support growth by decentralizing authority and encouraging collaboration. Whether through rotating team leads, cross-functional committees, or empowered project groups, these models create real-world opportunities for individuals to lead within a supportive framework. They also teach humility and cooperation, as leadership becomes about influence and contribution rather than hierarchy and control.

Developing leadership also requires robust mentorship systems. Mentorship provides structure, feedback, and accountability. A mentor offers guidance rooted in experience, while also empowering mentees to find their own voice. In successful mentorship relationships, both parties grow—mentors are challenged to reflect and articulate, while mentees are encouraged to stretch and innovate. Organizations that formalize mentorship create continuity, community, and a stronger leadership pipeline.

Communication is a core leadership skill that must be intentionally taught. Effective leaders know how to convey vision, inspire others, and listen actively. Communication is not merely about delivering information—it's about forging connection and building trust. Workshops, coaching, and intentional feedback loops help develop leaders who can navigate difficult conversations, resolve conflict, and align teams around shared goals. Another foundational aspect of leadership is emotional intelligence.

Leaders who are self-aware, emotionally regulated, and empathetic make better decisions and foster healthier cultures. Training in emotional intelligence—through assessments, simulations, and reflection—enables individuals to become more conscious of their behaviors and their impact on others. As emotional intelligence improves, so too does the capacity for inclusive, thoughtful, and sustained leadership. Cultivating leadership also requires creating space for innovation and experimentation. When individuals are encouraged to take initiative and try new approaches, they engage with greater purpose.

Innovation thrives in cultures where failure is viewed as feedback, and where leaders support exploration. Providing stretch assignments, innovation labs, or pilot projects allows individuals to lead through doing, learning, and iterating. Resilience is a hallmark of great leadership. Leaders are often called upon in times of uncertainty, stress, or change. Teaching resilience means helping individuals develop coping mechanisms, reflective practices, and support systems.

Training in growth mindset, mindfulness, and stress management strengthens not only individual leaders but the teams they support. Resilient leaders foster resilient communities. One powerful method for developing leadership at every level is through project-based experiences. Real-world leadership is tested not in theory, but in action. Projects that challenge individuals to plan, coordinate, and execute initiatives provide invaluable growth opportunities.

Whether it's organizing a school event, leading a community campaign, or managing a department improvement effort, these projects become leadership laboratories. Leadership must also be values-driven. Individuals must be encouraged to articulate their personal values and align them with organizational principles. When values drive behavior, leaders act with integrity, inspire loyalty, and create cultures of trust. Organizations should include values exploration in leadership training, helping individuals identify what matters most and how that shapes their actions.

Feedback is a vital part of leadership development. Effective leaders seek feedback regularly, respond without defensiveness, and model how to use it for growth. Peer feedback sessions, 360-degree reviews, and self-reflection tools help cultivate leaders who are humble, teachable, and responsive. Feedback-rich environments drive continuous improvement. Leadership is sustained through reflection.

Leaders must be given time and space to think. Journaling, coaching, retreats, and structured dialogue help leaders reconnect with their purpose, assess their impact, and plan for growth. Reflection transforms experience into wisdom and prevents burnout by reconnecting leaders with their core motivations. To develop leadership at every level, organizations must embed leadership in their systems. This includes recruitment, onboarding, professional development, evaluation, and recognition.

Leadership development cannot be a side program—it must be part of the fabric of the institution. Embedding leadership into performance expectations and reward systems signals its importance and supports consistency. Equity must be at the forefront of leadership development. Traditional leadership models often reflect privilege and exclusivity. A true culture of leadership must be inclusive, affirming diverse voices and perspectives.

This means actively seeking out underrepresented leaders, addressing systemic barriers, and creating culturally responsive leadership pathways. Inclusive leadership is not just ethical—it is effective. Leadership can be cultivated through storytelling. When individuals hear the leadership journeys of their peers, they are inspired to believe in their own capacity. Storytelling also humanizes leaders, making leadership feel accessible and relatable.

Including storytelling in training, staff meetings, and community events reinforces culture and builds connection. Collaboration is a critical leadership skill. In today's interconnected world, few initiatives succeed through individual effort alone. Leaders must learn to foster partnerships, navigate group dynamics, and align teams toward common goals. Team-based simulations, collaborative planning, and co-facilitation opportunities all provide fertile ground for developing collaboration.

Leadership is also shaped by cultural competence. Leaders at every level must understand the cultural contexts in which they operate. They must communicate respectfully across differences and lead with cultural humility. Training in cultural intelligence, bias awareness, and inclusive communication equips leaders to serve diverse teams and communities effectively. Sustainability in leadership requires succession planning.

Organizations must prepare for the future by identifying, nurturing, and preparing the next generation of leaders. Succession planning includes talent mapping, leadership apprenticeships, and knowledge transfer systems. When transitions are anticipated and supported, leadership is continuous rather than fragile. Creating a leadership culture means recognizing leadership in all forms. Not all leaders are extroverted or outspoken.

Some lead through relationships, others through creativity, others through quiet diligence. Celebrating diverse leadership styles affirms individuality and expands participation. No one should be excluded from leadership simply because they don't fit a narrow mold. To cultivate leadership at every level, accountability must be redefined. Rather than being rooted in punishment or performance metrics, accountability should be viewed as a shared commitment to excellence.

Leaders hold each other accountable through mutual trust, shared goals, and transparent dialogue. Accountability becomes a way of lifting each other up. Organizations and communities thrive when leadership becomes a way of life. When everyone sees themselves as capable of influence, responsibility, and contribution, possibilities expand. People begin to ask, "What can I do?" rather than "What is someone else doing?" This mindset shift unleashes collective energy and transforms passive environments into dynamic ecosystems of growth.

Leadership is not just about what we do—it's about who we become. Developing leaders at every level means developing character. Patience, empathy, courage, humility, and discipline are all leadership traits that must be cultivated over time. Leadership programs must include not just competencies, but character formation. As leadership is cultivated broadly, the organization becomes more adaptive.

Change becomes less disruptive and more integrated. Innovation flows from every corner. People speak up with confidence, challenge respectfully, and collaborate eagerly. Leadership becomes a shared rhythm, not a top-down command. In education, business, and community life, the call is clear: we need more leaders, not fewer.

And we need them everywhere—not just at the top. Cultivating leadership at every level is not a luxury or an extra. It is a necessity for transformation, resilience, and equity. It is the foundation of progress that lasts. In the end, leadership development is people development.

It's about recognizing human potential and creating the conditions for it to flourish. When we commit to developing leaders at every level, we don't just grow organizations—we grow people. And that is the most powerful legacy any leader can leave behind.

Chapter 4: Purpose-Driven Planning

Purpose-driven planning is the cornerstone of impactful leadership. It ensures that every action, initiative, and decision aligns with a broader mission. Leaders who engage in purpose-driven planning are not simply reacting to the day's demands—they are crafting intentional strategies that serve long-term goals and values. This kind of planning does more than organize time; it shapes culture and drives legacy. When leaders begin with purpose, they begin with clarity. Purpose answers the why behind every what.

It motivates action and provides a filter for decision-making. A school leader, for instance, may plan the academic year not simply to meet compliance requirements but to ensure that each instructional day supports literacy growth, student engagement, and teacher development. Purpose gives weight and direction to planning. Vision is the natural companion of purpose. Vision stretches the imagination to what could be, while purpose grounds that vision in what must be.

Purpose-driven planners start by asking, 'What future are we creating, and why does it matter?' They visualize the desired impact and then reverse-engineer their strategies from that vision. This ensures their plans are proactive and principled, not reactive or disjointed. One of the essential skills of a purpose-driven planner is goal alignment. Goals should serve a clear purpose and not exist in isolation. SMART goals (Specific, Measurable, Achievable, Relevant, Time-bound) are most powerful when they are also mission-aligned.

Leaders must constantly evaluate: Does this goal support our core mission? If not, is it worth pursuing? This evaluation helps prevent goal clutter and ensures strategic coherence. Time management takes on a deeper meaning when driven by purpose. Every meeting, task, and initiative becomes an investment in the vision.

Leaders should perform time audits to ensure their calendars reflect their priorities. If a leader values team development but spends no time coaching staff, there's a misalignment. Purpose-driven time management requires courage: to say no to distractions and yes to what matters most. Purpose-driven planning also requires clarity of values. Before deciding what to do, leaders must decide what they stand for.

Values guide how plans are executed and how results are interpreted. Two organizations might have the same strategic plan on paper, but their culture will differ dramatically based on their values. Purpose anchors those values into the planning process, making the invisible visible. In educational settings, purpose-driven planning means putting students at the center of every decision. It means asking: How does this policy affect our most vulnerable learners?

How does this schedule support literacy growth? How do our assessments reflect real learning? When the purpose is student success—not mere compliance—the planning process becomes dynamic, responsive, and ethical. Leaders must also engage in data-informed purpose planning. Purpose gives direction, but data gives evidence.

An effective leader studies patterns in behavior, performance, and engagement to understand where gaps exist and how best to close them. Data becomes not just a score, but a story—a way to measure alignment between intention and outcome. Purpose-driven planning is inherently collaborative. It invites voices from across the organization to shape priorities and timelines. This shared ownership increases commitment and generates ideas that may otherwise be missed.

Inclusive planning processes build trust, reduce resistance, and reflect the lived experience of those the plan will impact. Flexibility is another hallmark of purpose-driven planning. While the vision remains constant, the path to that vision may shift. Leaders must be willing to pivot based on new insights, challenges, or opportunities. Rigid plans can break under pressure, but purpose-driven plans bend and adapt without losing their direction.

Long-term planning should be broken into short-term wins. Milestones provide momentum and opportunities for reflection. Each win reinforces the plan's purpose and helps build credibility. Leaders should celebrate progress and use these celebrations to renew commitment to the larger goal. Purpose is sustained through intentional moments of acknowledgment.

Reflection must be built into every planning cycle. After an initiative is completed, leaders should ask: Did we fulfill our purpose? What worked, and what didn't? How can we refine our next plan? Reflection transforms planning from a one-time event into a continuous cycle of learning and growth.

Leaders must also plan for legacy. Purpose is not confined to short-term results; it asks what impact will endure. Legacy planning includes mentoring successors, documenting processes, and creating systems that outlast any one leader. Purpose-driven planning is inherently selfless—it seeks impact that transcends personal recognition. Equity is a critical lens in purpose-driven planning.

Without intentional effort, plans may unintentionally reinforce disparities. Leaders must analyze who benefits from each plan, whose voices are missing, and how resources are allocated. Equity audits, community engagement, and culturally responsive practices ensure that purpose is inclusive and justice-centered. Technology can support or derail purpose-driven planning depending on how it's used.

Tools like digital calendars, project management apps, and dashboards can enhance visibility and accountability.

However, leaders must be cautious not to confuse efficiency with effectiveness. Technology should serve purpose—not replace it. Leaders should also plan for wellbeing. A sustainable plan considers the emotional and physical health of the team. Burnout is often a symptom of purpose misalignment.

When people are overworked on tasks that feel meaningless, energy wanes. Purpose-driven planners ensure that initiatives are paced thoughtfully, with built-in supports and boundaries. A leader's personal purpose must align with the organizational mission. When these are in harmony, planning becomes energizing. When they are misaligned, planning feels forced.

Leaders should periodically revisit their own calling: Why do I lead? What am I hoping to create in the world? This introspection ensures authenticity and joy in the work. Crisis situations test the strength of purpose-driven planning. In moments of chaos, purpose becomes the compass.

Plans may need to change overnight, but purpose remains. Leaders who have internalized their 'why' can make quick, ethical decisions and guide others with confidence. Purpose brings calm and conviction during storms. Communication is vital in sustaining purpose. A great plan, poorly communicated, is a lost opportunity.

Leaders must articulate not just what the plan is, but why it matters. Storytelling, visual roadmaps, and transparent updates help align everyone with the shared purpose. When people understand the why, they are more invested in the how. Leaders should plan with an eye on the community. Purpose that ignores stakeholders becomes self-serving.

Community engagement ensures that planning reflects lived experiences and local wisdom. Listening sessions, surveys, and partnerships make planning a shared journey, not a solo endeavor. Interdisciplinary thinking enriches purpose-driven planning. Combining insights from education, business, psychology, and the arts allows leaders to design innovative solutions. Creativity is not separate from purpose—it amplifies it.

Purpose-driven plans are not only sound; they are soulful and imaginative. Planning also requires courage. Purpose may lead a leader to make unpopular decisions, challenge the status quo, or speak hard truths. Purpose-driven leaders are not reckless, but they are brave. They know that real change requires discomfort and that short-term resistance is worth long-term impact.

Metrics must align with purpose. It is easy to measure what's convenient rather than what's meaningful. Leaders must design evaluation tools that reflect their true goals—whether that's student growth, community trust, or team collaboration. Misaligned metrics distort progress and demoralize teams. Accountability should be reframed as commitment to purpose.

Rather than being punitive, accountability becomes about integrity. Leaders ask themselves and others: Are we doing what we said we would do? Are we staying true to our purpose? This culture of accountability fuels honesty, transparency, and excellence. Finally, purpose-driven planning is an act of hope.

It says: The future can be better, and we have a role in creating it. It invites imagination, determination, and unity. When leaders plan with purpose, they plant seeds of transformation that will blossom long after their tenure ends. Purpose-driven planning fosters a results-oriented mindset that goes beyond checking boxes. It ensures that initiatives produce measurable, lasting impact aligned with a leader's long-term vision.

Leaders who adopt this mindset think critically about which activities drive value and which may simply occupy time without delivering meaningful outcomes. This kind of planning requires asking hard questions, setting clear benchmarks, and staying relentlessly focused on the deeper 'why' behind each action. The strategic use of time reflects a leader's sense of purpose. Time is not merely scheduled—it is stewarded. Leaders must distinguish between urgent and important, creating systems that prioritize what sustains growth over what demands immediate attention.

Purpose-driven time blocking, goal batching, and agenda setting all help protect time for what truly matters. Team development is a critical component of purpose-driven planning. A leader's purpose is amplified through the people they support. Purposeful plans include space for coaching, collaboration, and skill-building. These investments transform average teams into high-performing cultures rooted in trust, innovation, and shared responsibility.

Leaders should view budgeting as a moral document. Purpose-driven financial planning allocates resources in ways that reflect the organization's mission. Dollars become tools for impact, not just balance sheets. When budgets are created through a purpose lens, every expenditure is seen as a statement of values. Leaders must ask: Are we funding what we say we value?

Cultural alignment enhances purpose-driven efforts. Plans must resonate with the lived experiences, beliefs, and traditions of the people they serve. Leaders who ignore culture risk disengagement and resistance. Those who embrace culture build credibility, foster ownership, and catalyze innovation through cultural fluency. The language of planning also matters.

Purpose-driven leaders choose words that inspire, clarify, and unify. Vague goals like 'improve performance' are replaced with bold declarations: 'Increase student voice in curriculum design by 50%.' Specific, inspiring language mobilizes action and reduces ambiguity. Scalable planning is another trait of purpose-driven leadership. Plans must be designed to grow with the organization without losing focus. This requires modular strategies—pilot programs, replicable models, and knowledge documentation—that allow innovation to scale sustainably.

Scalability ensures that impact is not isolated but multiplied. A commitment to purpose also requires ethical foresight. Leaders must consider the long-term consequences of short-term decisions. This means anticipating unintended impacts, including equity gaps, environmental consequences, or burnout. Purpose provides a lens through which leaders forecast risks and build plans with integrity.

Resilient systems are part of purpose-driven planning. Leaders cannot plan only for the ideal; they must build in redundancy and recovery strategies. Whether through cross-training, crisis protocols, or backup workflows, these systems ensure continuity of purpose even in the face of disruption. Community partnerships deepen the effectiveness of planning. Purpose grows when shared.

Leaders should engage nonprofits, businesses, families, and faith organizations in co-designing initiatives that reflect collective values. These partnerships provide resources, insight, and accountability that single entities often lack. Intergenerational planning elevates purpose across time. Wise leaders consider how today's actions will shape future generations. In education, this means preparing students not just for tests, but for life.

In business, it means building sustainable practices that outlast trends. Legacy planning demands a long view and a deep sense of stewardship. Leadership teams benefit from regular purpose audits. These audits involve examining whether current practices reflect stated values and strategic goals. If a school claims to value inclusion but its data shows discipline disparities, the audit becomes a tool for realignment.

Purpose audits promote honesty and recalibration. The most effective plans are those that are revisited and refined frequently. Quarterly reviews, stakeholder feedback loops, and reflective retreats help leaders keep their purpose front and center. These checkpoints prevent drift and reinvigorate the team with a sense of shared mission. Visualization is a powerful purpose-alignment tool.

Leaders can create vision boards, dashboards, or thematic maps that connect goals with impact. These visuals act as reminders, aligning teams around key objectives and showing the narrative behind the numbers. Cross-functional integration strengthens purpose. When departments or initiatives operate in silos, planning becomes fragmented. Purpose-driven leaders create connective tissue between teams—through joint meetings, shared goals, and open communication—to ensure alignment and synergy.

Mentorship and leadership development should be woven into every plan. A sustainable purpose cannot rely on a single visionary—it must be distributed. Intentional succession planning and growth pipelines ensure that the mission continues even as personnel shifts. Environmental sustainability can also be integrated into purpose-driven plans. Leaders who value long-term impact consider the ecological footprint of their initiatives.

Greener procurement, energy efficiency, and conservation education all align planning with a purpose that includes the planet. Purpose-driven planning is not about perfection—it is about authenticity. Leaders must be willing to admit when something isn't working and course-correct. Vulnerability, honesty, and courage to fail forward are marks of purpose-led leadership. These qualities foster trust and innovation.

Celebration is part of sustaining purpose. Recognizing milestones, affirming contributions, and storytelling success remind the team why the work matters. Rituals of recognition connect people emotionally to the mission and prevent purpose fatigue. Ultimately, purpose-driven planning turns good intentions into great outcomes. It connects dreams with discipline, vision with action.

Leaders who plan with purpose leave a mark not just through what they build, but through how they inspire others to build as well. Reflection in planning is not a solitary act; it must be institutionalized. Purpose-driven organizations build reflection into meeting agendas, project debriefs, and quarterly retreats. These moments aren't just about evaluating what was done, but why it was done and how it advanced the mission. Reflection deepens commitment to purpose by transforming experience into learning.

Leaders should ensure that plans are co-authored by those who will implement them. Too often, strategic plans are created at the top and handed down. Purpose is diluted when voices are excluded. By involving stakeholders from multiple levels—teachers, students, parents, and frontline staff—leaders create ownership, generate stronger ideas, and build collective purpose. Scenario planning is another strategic tool in the purpose-driven leader's arsenal.

This approach asks: What could happen, and how will we respond? It builds flexibility and foresight into the planning process. Whether preparing for a budget shortfall, staff turnover, or external crisis, scenario planning ensures that purpose can remain intact even under pressure. Leaders must guard against mission drift. As organizations grow, they may be tempted by funding opportunities or partnerships that aren't fully aligned with their purpose.

While adaptability is important, it should not come at the cost of integrity. Purpose-driven leaders regularly revisit the mission to ensure that every new opportunity supports the greater goal. Planning for purpose means planning for people. Organizational change happens at the speed of trust. Leaders must intentionally include capacity-building for team members in their strategic designs.

This includes training, mentorship, wellness supports, and voice in decision-making. Empowered people become the strongest executors of purposeful plans. Assessment and evaluation should be formative, not just summative. In a purpose-driven system, feedback loops are designed to improve, not just to prove. This means engaging in regular checkpoints, formative assessments, and iterative processes.

When teams feel safe to reflect and adapt, they grow more connected to the mission. A plan without clarity is just a wish list. Purpose-driven planning requires clarity of goals, roles, timelines, and resources. Everyone involved must know what success looks like, what their responsibilities are, and what supports they can expect. Clarity reduces confusion and creates confidence, allowing people to act with boldness and alignment.

Visual thinking tools help bring plans to life. Whether it's Gantt charts, Kanban boards, logic models, or infographics, visualizations make strategy concrete. They help teams grasp the flow of action, understand dependencies, and connect their daily tasks to overarching goals. A clear picture of the plan keeps purpose visible and top-of-mind. Interpersonal dynamics shape the planning environment.

A culture of psychological safety encourages candor, risk-taking, and innovation. Purpose-driven leaders model vulnerability, invite dissent, and create spaces where disagreement can lead to discovery. The healthiest plans emerge from teams where truth can be spoken in love. Digital transformation must align with purpose. As schools, nonprofits, and companies digitize, the goal should not be efficiency alone.

Purpose should guide tech adoption, ensuring that tools amplify impact rather than distract from it. Leaders must ask: Does this technology make us better at living our mission? Consistency builds credibility. When people see that leadership follows through on purposeful plans, trust grows. Consistency in communication, decision-making, and follow-up signals integrity.

It creates a virtuous cycle: teams invest more when they believe that plans are more than just talk. Leaders must confront complexity with curiosity. Purpose-driven planning does not seek to oversimplify, but to make meaning from complexity. Systems thinking helps leaders understand how different parts of an organization interact. This big-picture approach allows for coordinated action and avoids the trap of solving isolated symptoms rather than root causes.

Celebration is not an afterthought—it is a strategic action. Purpose is sustained when people see the fruits of their labor. Regular celebrations, whether formal or informal, remind teams why their work matters. These moments of joy replenish energy, strengthen bonds, and invite others to join the mission. Purpose thrives in an environment of gratitude.

Acknowledging effort, progress, and presence helps reinforce shared values. Leaders who express gratitude regularly create a culture where people feel seen and valued. Gratitude shifts the tone from obligation to opportunity and deepens emotional investment in purposeful work. Leaders must also plan for disruption—not just as a possibility, but as a certainty. Whether it's a global crisis, leadership change, or policy shift, disruptions test the integrity of purpose.

By embedding adaptability and values-based decision-making into every level of planning, leaders can navigate the unknown without losing their way. Stakeholder mapping is a practical tool in purpose-driven planning. Leaders identify who is affected by the plan, who has influence, and who can help drive implementation. Clear stakeholder strategies—through engagement, communication, and coalition-building—amplify both reach and relevance. Personal purpose must be renewed as part of the leadership cycle.

Leaders should regularly revisit their own 'why'—the inner conviction that called them to this work. This renewal can happen through journaling, spiritual practices, coaching, or time in nature. When leaders operate from a clear sense of self, their plans radiate authenticity. Cross-cultural leadership planning expands the lens of purpose. In a global or diverse context, leaders must consider how cultural identities shape experience, expectation, and expression.

Culturally responsive planning honors this richness by integrating diverse ways of knowing and leading into the strategy. Purposeful plans should include rituals—anchor moments that reinforce the mission. These might include opening meetings with a mission story, recognizing a student's growth, or ending the week with a reflection circle. Rituals build rhythm, create meaning, and bring the team back to purpose. Finally, purpose-driven planning must make room for boldness.

Safe plans may be easier to execute, but they rarely inspire. Purpose pushes leaders to dream bigger, risk failure, and lead transformation. The most powerful plans are those rooted in values, shaped by vision, and executed with fearless intent. In purpose-driven planning, the language used in strategy documents and communication materials plays a critical role in driving alignment and motivation. Every word either supports clarity or creates confusion.

Leaders should avoid jargon and prioritize accessible, inclusive language that resonates across teams and stakeholder groups. This promotes transparency and reinforces a shared understanding of goals. Leaders must plan for emotional intelligence as part of their strategic priorities. Emotional awareness, empathy, and regulation are essential leadership traits that shape team dynamics and organizational health. Incorporating training and development focused on emotional intelligence enhances collaboration and reduces conflict, ultimately keeping the team aligned with its core mission.

One of the most overlooked aspects of purpose-driven planning is the leader's ability to practice self-care. Sustainable leadership begins with well-being. If a leader is chronically burned out or detached, their planning becomes reactive and transactional. Purposeful leaders design boundaries, renewal routines, and support systems that preserve their energy for the long haul. Interruption management is a vital skill for keeping plans on track.

Purpose-driven leaders anticipate distractions and design systems to minimize their impact. This includes limiting unnecessary meetings, establishing quiet work periods, and empowering team members to solve problems independently when appropriate. Protecting the planning process from constant disruption maintains momentum and quality. Effective succession planning also reflects purpose. Leaders must plan not just for their legacy, but for the ongoing leadership of their mission.

Identifying, mentoring, and preparing future leaders ensures that the vision does not fade with a single transition. Purposeful succession embeds values and strategy into the organization's DNA. An often underestimated aspect of planning is decision latency—the lag between identifying a need and acting on it. Purpose-driven planning reduces decision latency by creating clear criteria for action and empowering decentralized decision-making. This increases agility while preserving strategic coherence.

Psychological safety is not just a cultural ideal; it's a planning imperative. Plans are only as strong as the candor they attract. When team members feel safe to raise concerns, question assumptions, or share early feedback, leaders can adjust before problems escalate. This transparency strengthens both process and outcomes. Purpose-driven leaders take time to define success in behavioral terms.

Rather than focusing solely on outcomes, they identify what actions and mindsets signal alignment with the mission. This allows for earlier course correction and a more holistic view of organizational health. Behavioral clarity reinforces strategic focus. One hallmark of mature planning is the ability to balance innovation with tradition. Leaders must know when to honor legacy systems and when to challenge them.

Purpose becomes the measuring stick: Does this practice still serve our mission? If so, refine it. If not, reimagine it. Incorporating design thinking into planning brings a user-centered, iterative lens to strategy. This approach encourages leaders to empathize with those affected by the plan, prototype solutions, gather feedback, and revise continuously.

Design thinking ensures that plans remain grounded in real-world insight and remain responsive to change. Purpose-driven planning often results in a narrative—a storyline that communicates where the organization has been, where it is going, and why it matters. This narrative builds cohesion and helps internal and external stakeholders see themselves in the journey. Leaders should cultivate storytelling as a strategic asset. Microplanning, or the ability to plan in smaller iterative cycles, is critical for flexibility.

Large-scale annual plans can become obsolete quickly in fast-changing environments. Purpose-driven leaders use weekly and monthly sprints to test ideas, evaluate impact, and make rapid adjustments without losing alignment to the overarching vision. Inclusion planning is distinct from general collaboration. It involves intentionally bringing in marginalized voices, designing equity checkpoints, and creating pathways for systemic participation. This form of purpose planning ensures justice is woven into the structure, not simply addressed at the surface.

Redundancy is a principle borrowed from engineering that supports resilience in leadership. Purposeful plans should have backups—whether in staffing, technology, or strategy. This doesn't imply inefficiency; rather, it reflects preparation. When one element fails, the mission continues because purpose has multiple supports. The feedback process itself should be structured with care.

Generic surveys and surface-level check-ins do little to strengthen plans. Purpose-driven feedback involves specific, open-ended prompts that tie responses to the strategic goals. Leaders should create multiple feedback loops across time and roles. Values clarification exercises should precede planning whenever possible. These can take the form of group discussions, ranking exercises, or individual journaling.

When people are clear about their values, they make better decisions, commit more deeply to goals, and find personal meaning in collective outcomes. Agile methodologies can be a strong complement to purpose. While often associated with software development, agile frameworks—short cycles, regular reviews, team autonomy—fit well in purpose-driven contexts where responsiveness and iteration are key. Leaders should adapt agile elements to fit their culture and strategy. Clarity in roles and responsibilities prevents mission dilution.

When everyone knows not just what they're doing, but how it contributes to the larger purpose, there is less friction, more collaboration, and greater efficiency. Leaders should define and communicate roles clearly within each plan. Well-crafted mission statements are more than slogans. They are compact expressions of purpose that serve as a decision-making compass. Leaders should reference the mission often, revisit its language annually, and test decisions against it.

A mission that is alive in daily practice keeps strategy aligned and vibrant. A plan without ongoing leadership development is shortsighted. Purpose requires continual personal and professional growth. Leaders should include training pathways, peer coaching, and experiential learning in their planning process. When teams grow, the mission advances faster and with deeper commitment.

Purpose-driven planning is ultimately a human endeavor. It combines vision with strategy, hope with discipline, and inspiration with execution. It demands that leaders bring their full selves to the task—not just as administrators, but as architects of meaningful impact. Every plan is an opportunity to express what matters most and to make it real in the lives of others. One of the foundational practices in purpose-driven planning is the inclusion of ethical checkpoints.

These checkpoints serve as moments of pause within the plan where leaders ask: Does this step align with our values? Are we unintentionally harming a group we intend to serve? By embedding ethics throughout the planning stages, leaders protect their mission from drifting into unintended consequences. In education, for instance, purpose-driven lesson planning involves more than standards alignment or assessment preparation. It includes designing learning experiences that spark curiosity, honor student identities, and build transferable skills.

Purpose changes the question from 'What should students learn?' to 'What kind of thinkers and contributors are we shaping?' This philosophical shift transforms classrooms into communities of growth. Strategic pacing is another underestimated aspect of impactful planning. A well-paced plan accounts for energy levels, seasonal rhythms, and team capacity. It prevents burnout by balancing urgency with rest. Leaders who respect the human element of planning are more likely to sustain momentum and retain talent over the long term.

Feedback must flow vertically and horizontally within an organization. It's not enough for team members to evaluate leaders or for departments to self-assess. True alignment emerges when feedback crosses silos, levels, and perspectives. Leaders should institutionalize cross-functional review cycles to ensure plans are tested from multiple vantage points. Another key is embedding adaptability into the plan itself.

Rather than designing rigid, unchangeable roadmaps, purpose-driven planners build in choice points—pre-designated opportunities to revisit assumptions, gather new input, and iterate forward. This ensures that the plan remains a living document rather than a static obligation. Benchmarking against purpose-aligned organizations can offer clarity and motivation. Leaders should look beyond their own walls to observe how other mission-driven entities structure their planning, engage stakeholders, and measure success. These comparisons can offer both inspiration and cautionary tales to guide planning decisions.

Clear documentation is the bridge between intention and action. Purposeful plans must be communicated not only through meetings but through well-organized documents, workflows, and timelines. This clarity empowers team members to execute independently and fosters shared understanding across departments and generations. Purpose must extend to the language used in performance reviews. When evaluations are tied back to the organization's mission, they shift from punitive reports to development opportunities.

Purpose-driven leaders provide feedback with the intent to re-align, encourage, and reinforce the deeper 'why' behind daily work. In any planning process, tension will arise between idealism and realism. Leaders must embrace this tension rather than avoid it. The ideal points to the highest vision of what's possible; realism anchors that vision in current constraints. The interplay between the two sharpens strategy and increases the chances of sustainable success.

Finally, true purpose-driven planning demands love—not in a sentimental sense, but as a deep care for people, for outcomes, and for the world we hope to shape. Love animates purpose, deepens accountability, and inspires resilience. Plans rooted in love do more than check boxes—they change lives and leave legacies.

Chapter 5: The Power of Relationships

At the core of every successful leadership journey lies the power of relationships. Whether in education, business, or community engagement, meaningful relationships serve as the foundation upon which trust, growth, and collaboration are built. Leaders who prioritize relationship-building foster environments where people feel seen, heard, and valued. These emotional anchors enable teams to perform not only with competence but with commitment. Relationships in leadership are not merely a byproduct of time spent together—they are the result of intentional investment. This includes active listening, consistent presence, authentic empathy, and a willingness to engage in difficult conversations.

When leaders treat relationships as strategic assets rather than peripheral niceties, they unlock higher engagement, deeper loyalty, and more creative problem-solving across their organizations. Emotional intelligence is a cornerstone of relational leadership. The ability to recognize one's own emotions, manage them effectively, and navigate interpersonal dynamics with sensitivity allows leaders to build stronger connections. This is particularly important in moments of stress, conflict, or transition, when trust may be tested and clarity is critical. In education, the teacher-student relationship is often the single greatest predictor of student success.

When students believe their teachers care about them as individuals, they become more motivated, more resilient, and more willing to take academic risks. Similarly, when school leaders cultivate strong relationships with staff, morale improves and performance flourishes. Authentic relationships are built on mutual respect. Leaders must resist the temptation to engage with others solely for what they can gain. Instead, they should cultivate curiosity about others' experiences, acknowledge their contributions, and invest in their growth.

This approach humanizes leadership and strengthens collective purpose. One of the most powerful tools a leader can wield is the art of recognition. Public and private affirmations—whether verbal praise, handwritten notes, or formal awards—reinforce relational bonds and signal appreciation. Recognition fosters motivation, enhances retention, and promotes a culture of gratitude that ripples across teams. Consistency is a hallmark of strong relational leadership.

People trust leaders who show up the same way over time—not because they are unchanging, but because their values and behavior align. Consistency builds psychological safety, allowing people to take risks, admit mistakes, and ask for help without fear of judgment. Boundaries are also essential in healthy leadership relationships. Respecting the line between professional expectations and personal autonomy ensures that relationships remain ethical and sustainable. Leaders who model and respect boundaries create environments that honor well-being and reduce burnout.

Relational leadership requires vulnerability. Leaders must be willing to share their own challenges, admit when they are wrong, and ask for support. This authenticity invites reciprocity, encouraging others to do the same. Vulnerability does not weaken a leader's influence—it deepens it. Trust is the currency of leadership relationships.

It is built through transparency, follow-through, and honesty. Broken trust can derail even the most well-designed strategies, while strong trust can transform ordinary teams into extraordinary ones. Leaders should prioritize trust-building not as a task to check off, but as a daily practice woven into every interaction. Mentorship is a powerful extension of relational leadership. When experienced professionals take the time to invest in emerging leaders, they create a legacy of growth and wisdom.

Effective mentors provide not only guidance, but also encouragement and challenge. They offer perspective gained through experience and help mentees avoid common pitfalls. Mentorship fosters a culture of learning that strengthens the entire organization. Collaboration is fueled by strong relationships. When individuals trust one another, they are more likely to share ideas, challenge assumptions, and co-create solutions.

Collaborative environments emerge when leaders foster respect, curiosity, and psychological safety. These cultures of mutual respect allow people to lean into discomfort and embrace innovation as a team rather than in silos. Communication plays a central role in building and maintaining relationships. Leaders must communicate with clarity, intention, and care. This includes not just what is said, but how it is said.

Tone, timing, and delivery can transform a difficult message into a constructive one. Listening is equally important. Leaders who truly listen gain valuable insight and build trust through validation. In schools, community organizations, and businesses alike, building partnerships beyond the walls of the institution is key to success. Relationships with families, local leaders, civic organizations, and other stakeholders broaden the reach of a leader's impact.

These external relationships support resource sharing, alignment, and advocacy efforts that help organizations thrive. Conflict is an inevitable part of any relationship. What distinguishes great leaders is how they navigate that conflict. Purpose-driven leaders address tension directly and respectfully. They do not avoid difficult conversations but instead use them as opportunities for growth.

Conflict handled well strengthens relationships by demonstrating care, honesty, and mutual investment in resolution. Relationships rooted in shared purpose endure adversity. Teams that are connected by a deep belief in their mission are more likely to weather change, disappointment, and external pressure. Purpose acts as a compass that guides behavior, decision-making, and emotional regulation. When purpose is shared and clear, relationships become resilient.

Cultural competence is essential in today's diverse leadership contexts. Leaders must understand and honor the identities, traditions, and values of those they serve and work alongside. Relationship-building in multicultural environments requires humility, active listening, and a commitment to equity. Inclusive leadership creates belonging, and belonging fuels engagement. Celebrating team and individual milestones reinforces relational bonds.

Recognizing birthdays, work anniversaries, project completions, and personal achievements signals that people matter beyond their output. These moments of celebration foster connection and deepen loyalty. Leaders who notice and honor the humanity of their teams create cultures of care. Transparency is one of the most powerful tools in a leader's relational toolkit. Sharing the rationale behind decisions, being honest about limitations, and communicating clearly about expectations reduces ambiguity and builds confidence.

Even when news is difficult, people appreciate honesty delivered with empathy. Consistency between a leader's words and actions creates trust. When people observe alignment between what a leader says and does, they believe in their integrity. Integrity, in turn, deepens respect and fosters long-term commitment. Leaders who model ethical behavior shape organizational cultures rooted in accountability and care.

Leadership without relational depth is often transactional and short-lived. In contrast, relationships formed with intention and sustained with care become the channels through which influence flows most naturally. Leaders who make space for personal connection—not just professional exchange—develop trust that fuels transformation. Relationship-building also improves organizational agility. When strong relational ties exist, communication flows more easily, feedback is more readily given and received, and adaptation occurs more quickly.

People who trust each other don't need layers of bureaucracy to coordinate; they move in rhythm because of mutual respect and shared vision. Humility is another essential ingredient in building relationships. Leaders who admit when they don't have all the answers and who ask for help foster mutual growth and collaboration. Humility creates space for others to contribute their strengths, creating a more balanced and inclusive team dynamic. Cross-generational relationships offer unique benefits in leadership.

Veteran leaders bring wisdom and experience, while emerging leaders offer fresh perspectives and innovation. When relationships are cultivated across age groups, organizations enjoy a more dynamic, adaptive, and visionary culture that honors both history and progress. Mentorship goes both ways. Reverse mentorship—where younger or less experienced team members mentor more senior leaders—builds empathy, sharpens cultural awareness, and creates mutual respect. These relationships flatten hierarchies and strengthen innovation by creating a learning culture at every level.

Leaders must also build relationships with themselves. Self-awareness, self-reflection, and self-compassion are the foundation for healthy external relationships. A leader who knows their own values, triggers, and emotional needs is better equipped to engage others with integrity and insight. Relationship-building takes time, and leaders must be patient with the process. Trust is not built in a single meeting or email—it is cultivated through dozens of small moments, over time.

Leaders who show up consistently, honor their word, and make space for others' stories earn trust slowly but surely. In community settings, relationship-building is the bridge to equity and justice. Leaders who build relationships with underserved populations demonstrate their commitment not just to outcomes, but to belonging. These relationships are not extractive or transactional—they are rooted in mutual dignity and shared future. Technology, when used intentionally, can enhance relationship-building.

Video calls, messaging apps, and collaborative platforms allow teams to stay connected across distances. However, technology should not replace in-person connection when possible. The warmth of face-to-face interaction cannot be fully replicated digitally. Leadership presence is deeply tied to relational power. Presence means more than physical availability—it includes emotional attentiveness, engagement in conversation, and a commitment to being fully in the moment.

Leaders who cultivate presence earn relational credibility and serve as anchors in times of uncertainty. One powerful way leaders build relationships is through storytelling. Sharing personal experiences, challenges, and turning points creates emotional resonance. Stories make leaders relatable, demystify authority, and inspire others to connect their own journey to a shared mission. A compelling story builds bridges between roles, generations, and perspectives.

Relational leadership thrives in organizations that practice shared leadership. When decision-making is distributed and voices are honored at every level, relationships grow stronger. Shared leadership shifts the focus from hierarchy to partnership, creating a culture where collaboration and co-ownership are the norm. Trust deepens when leaders follow through on promises. Small commitments, such as being on time or delivering feedback when promised, build a track record of reliability.

Over time, this consistency communicates respect and fosters psychological safety, empowering others to lead boldly and authentically. The power of relationships extends to crisis management. In moments of uncertainty or conflict, teams that are relationally strong remain cohesive. Leaders who have cultivated strong relationships before a crisis find it easier to unify people, mobilize resources, and navigate high-stakes situations with integrity. Feedback becomes more meaningful in the context of strong relationships.

When individuals feel respected and valued, they are more likely to receive feedback openly and view it as a tool for growth. Leaders who prioritize relationships create environments where feedback becomes a form of care, not criticism. Celebrating diversity strengthens relationships by honoring the unique experiences and contributions of each individual. Inclusive leaders recognize and amplify the voices of those from underrepresented backgrounds. They ensure that everyone has a seat at the table and feels empowered to lead from their identity.

Empathy in leadership is more than understanding others' emotions—it is taking action to support their well-being. Empathetic leaders ask meaningful questions, respond with compassion, and adapt their leadership to support the needs of their team. Empathy deepens connection and motivates higher engagement. Relational capital is a strategic advantage. It leads to faster problem-solving, greater resilience, and increased innovation.

When relationships are prioritized, organizations become more agile and adaptive because information flows freely, collaboration is high, and trust cushions the impact of risk-taking. Leaders must also engage in reflective practices that examine how their relational approaches are working. Journaling, mentorship check-ins, and team listening sessions can all be tools for assessing the health of professional relationships. Reflection ensures that relationships do not become stagnant, but continue to evolve with intentional care. Finally, the power of relationships lies in their ability to humanize leadership.

In a world driven by performance metrics and digital transactions, genuine connection is a radical act. Leaders who prioritize relationships build more than just effective teams—they build communities where people thrive, grow, and lead with purpose. Another important aspect of relational leadership is intentional collaboration across departments and disciplines. Silos can isolate good ideas, reduce efficiency, and create unnecessary tension. Leaders who prioritize relationship-building actively foster cross-functional partnerships.

They encourage dialogue between teams, break down barriers, and champion a culture of shared success over isolated achievement. Gratitude practices are also central to nurturing positive relationships. Whether expressed through handwritten notes, verbal acknowledgments, or team-wide celebrations, gratitude reinforces relational bonds. Leaders who frequently express appreciation create a ripple effect that increases morale, boosts productivity, and fosters a stronger sense of community. Relationships are strengthened by transparency during change.

Change often triggers uncertainty, and leaders who are upfront about the reasons behind transitions, the challenges expected, and the vision ahead will earn greater trust. Honesty—even when difficult—fortifies relational trust and helps people stay anchored in the mission. Relational leadership includes empowering others. Delegating meaningful responsibilities, trusting team members to make decisions, and celebrating their contributions helps individuals feel ownership and purpose. Empowerment builds confidence and increases organizational capacity while deepening mutual respect between leaders and their teams.

Relational equity should also be considered—this is the accumulated history of positive, trust-building interactions between people. Leaders with high relational equity can challenge or redirect others without being perceived as authoritarian. They can rally people in a crisis and inspire confidence even in moments of ambiguity. Relational equity allows influence to be exercised with grace. The physical work environment also impacts relationships.

Spaces that promote collaboration—such as open work areas, gathering spaces, and common lounges—foster interaction and community. Leaders who design environments for connection send a powerful message: relationships are not incidental, they are essential. Community service projects can strengthen relationships both within and beyond the organization. When teams work together on service initiatives, they develop empathy, solidarity, and a sense of shared purpose. These experiences create lasting memories and reframe team identity around collective impact.

Conflict resolution is a learned skill, and leaders who invest in this ability can maintain relationships even through disagreement. Effective conflict resolution involves listening without defensiveness, seeking common ground, and prioritizing shared goals. Leaders who facilitate these conversations model maturity, courage, and care. Peer coaching is a practical method of relationship development. Through regular one-on-one sessions, peers can reflect on challenges, share successes, and offer encouragement.

Peer coaching normalizes vulnerability and helps team members see themselves as contributors to one another's growth, not just competitors or coworkers. Lastly, rituals play a powerful role in relationship-building. Weekly check-ins, opening circles, closing reflections, or even shared meals can create consistent relational rhythms. These rituals give people something to look forward to, create predictability in the emotional life of the team, and support connection over time. Leaders who build strong relationships understand the importance of psychological safety.

In a psychologically safe environment, team members feel free to express ideas, ask questions, and admit mistakes without fear of embarrassment or retaliation. This kind of environment fosters creativity, problem-solving, and a deeper sense of belonging among team members. Social capital is another essential outcome of relationship-building. Social capital refers to the resources and advantages gained through networks of trust and reciprocity. Leaders who cultivate a culture of generosity and collaboration increase the social capital of their teams, making them more resilient and effective in responding to challenges.

Strong relationships are also grounded in shared rituals of reflection. Whether through daily debriefs, weekly wins, or end-of-project reviews, reflection allows teams to learn from their experiences and strengthen their relational bonds. These practices give voice to lessons learned and allow space for collective gratitude and growth.

Respecting cultural and personality differences enhances relationship-building. Not everyone expresses connection the same way.

Some people value directness; others value subtlety. Some prefer group celebrations; others prefer quiet affirmations. Leaders who recognize and respond to these differences demonstrate emotional intelligence and inclusive leadership. Networking, often seen as a transactional act, becomes deeply meaningful when it is based on authentic relationship-building. Leaders who approach networking as a way to serve, support, and learn from others cultivate long-term professional relationships that yield mutual benefit and expand collective impact.

Leaders also benefit from establishing relational anchors—individuals or small groups with whom they share regular, trust-based dialogue. These anchors help leaders stay grounded, process decisions, and maintain perspective. A strong anchor can serve as a sounding board, accountability partner, and source of encouragement during difficult times. Leadership succession planning benefits from strong relationships as well. When teams are relationally healthy, potential successors emerge organically.

They are identified not only by their technical skills but also by their ability to connect with others, influence through trust, and uphold the organization's values. Healthy succession is a byproduct of healthy relationships. Accountability becomes more relational than punitive when strong connections exist. Instead of policing behavior, leaders guide performance by referring back to shared goals, team agreements, and mutual commitments. In this context, accountability strengthens relationships because it reinforces mutual respect and the belief that every member is essential to success.

Servant leadership epitomizes the power of relationships. Leaders who serve first and lead second demonstrate humility, care, and commitment. They put the needs of others above their own, and by doing so, they gain deep respect and loyalty. This approach transforms hierarchical dynamics and builds cultures of trust. Finally, relationships endure when leaders lead with intention.

Every interaction—whether it's a quick hallway conversation or a formal performance review—has the potential to either deepen or damage a relationship. Leaders who are intentional about being present, clear, and compassionate create the kind of relational ecosystems that sustain long-term success. The foundation of meaningful relationships in leadership is empathy. Empathy requires leaders to listen beyond words, perceive underlying emotions, and respond with care. It helps cultivate a sense of shared humanity in professional environments.

When leaders operate with empathy, they foster connections that transcend roles and titles. Relational intelligence—the ability to read social dynamics and adapt accordingly—is an advanced leadership skill. Unlike general emotional intelligence, relational intelligence focuses specifically on managing group dynamics, resolving interpersonal tension, and cultivating harmony within teams. Leaders with relational intelligence build lasting influence. Trust is continuously reinforced through consistency.

When leaders uphold the same standards for themselves that they expect from others, trust deepens. Trust is not a one-time achievement; it is a living currency that must be nourished with ongoing integrity and fairness. One overlooked element in relational leadership is fun. Leaders who intentionally incorporate play, humor, and joy into the workplace encourage connection. Shared laughter builds emotional bridges and alleviates stress.

It humanizes interactions and creates space for stronger bonds. Honoring people's names, pronouns, and identities is a small but powerful relational practice. It signals respect and intentionality. Leaders who pay attention to such details demonstrate that each person matters. This attentiveness contributes to a culture of dignity and psychological safety.

Celebrating relational wins—not just performance wins—is an emerging leadership practice. Recognizing moments when someone supported a peer, diffused a conflict, or offered emotional care reinforces values of community and connection. These relational celebrations affirm that how we succeed matters just as much as what we achieve. Peer-led initiatives foster horizontal relationships that reduce dependency on top-down leadership. When peers lead mentorship circles, innovation hubs, or affinity groups, relational leadership is democratized.

These grassroots structures strengthen the fabric of community within organizations. Inclusion begins with relationship. Leaders who build genuine relationships with marginalized individuals create openings for equity. These relationships cannot be symbolic or superficial; they must be built on trust, understanding, and shared commitment to justice. Relational proximity transforms good intentions into systemic change.

Listening sessions are tools for deepening organizational relationships. By hosting spaces where staff or stakeholders can voice concerns, aspirations, and feedback, leaders model humility and responsiveness. These sessions also highlight trends that may otherwise go unnoticed, allowing for proactive support and change. Leaders who engage in restorative practices strengthen their teams after relational harm has occurred. Restorative conversations aim not to assign blame but to rebuild trust and community.

These practices demonstrate that even after missteps, relationships can be repaired and strengthened through accountability and care. Leadership through relationships also includes showing up during times of personal hardship. A leader who reaches out during a team member's time of loss, illness, or struggle reinforces the message that people matter beyond their roles. This kind of support can forge bonds that carry through an entire career. Transparency around leadership intentions further strengthens relationships.

When team members understand not only what decisions are made but why they are made, they feel included in the process. This transparency builds alignment and fosters confidence, even when decisions are difficult or unpopular. Interpersonal grace—giving people the benefit of the doubt—is a relational practice that builds psychological safety. Not every mistake is a character flaw; sometimes it's a product of stress or miscommunication. Leaders who lead with grace deescalate tension and open space for accountability without shame.

Leaders should intentionally create opportunities for informal connection. Scheduled social time, walk-and-talk meetings, or casual check-ins help break down walls and deepen bonds. When connection is prioritized alongside productivity, teams grow in cohesion and creativity. Feedback loops between leaders and teams ensure that relationships are not one-sided. Leaders should not only give feedback but actively solicit it.

When feedback flows in both directions, relational equity is established, and trust is cultivated as part of everyday practice. Publicly advocating for team members in high-stakes or visible moments also strengthens relationships. When a leader credits a team member in a public meeting or defends their integrity under scrutiny, it affirms their value and builds loyalty. People remember the leaders who advocated for them. Relational leadership includes celebrating the process, not just the outcome.

Acknowledging the effort, collaboration, and challenges overcome reinforces a growth mindset and values the journey. This celebration of process strengthens bonds and keeps people engaged in their work. Leadership that prioritizes relationships is especially important in virtual and hybrid environments. Without hallway conversations or informal gatherings, leaders must be more intentional in checking in, fostering connection, and making space for informal engagement through digital tools. Relational fatigue can occur when leaders are stretched too thin or when boundaries are not maintained.

Leaders must replenish their own relational energy through rest, support networks, and personal reflection. Healthy leaders build healthier relationships. Ultimately, relationship-centered leadership creates cultures of care. These are environments where people feel safe, respected, and inspired. In such cultures, performance is not forced—it flows naturally from commitment, connection, and a shared sense of purpose.

Story circles can be used as a powerful tool to build deeper understanding and empathy among teams. In a story circle, each person is given the opportunity to share personal experiences around a central theme. These shared narratives create powerful emotional connections that strengthen team unity. Affirmations in leadership are often undervalued. Regularly acknowledging someone's character, effort, or growth—not just accomplishments—reinforces their sense of self-worth.

When people feel seen for who they are, not just what they do, their connection to the organization grows stronger. Community-building extends relational leadership beyond organizational boundaries. Leaders who initiate or participate in community events—such as volunteer days, public panels, or local forums—position their organizations as invested members of the larger social fabric. Trust-building in multicultural teams requires cultural humility. Leaders must be open to learning from cultures different from their own and be willing to adjust practices to be more inclusive.

Cultural humility helps avoid assumptions and demonstrates genuine respect for diverse backgrounds and worldviews. Relational leadership also requires a long view. Some relationships take years to fully develop and mature. Investing in people with no immediate expectation of return fosters goodwill and lays the groundwork for collaboration that can emerge at unexpected moments. Celebrating micro-wins keeps teams engaged and connected.

These small achievements—completing a difficult task, resolving a conflict, or taking initiative—deserve recognition. When leaders highlight micro-wins, they signal that every contribution matters. Leaders can build relationships by simply being accessible. Keeping an open-door policy, scheduling time for one-on-ones, or holding office hours sends a clear message: you are approachable and interested in what your team has to say. Accessibility nurtures trust and psychological safety.

Even in difficult conversations, relationships can be strengthened. When handled with respect and transparency, tough feedback moments or decisions about performance can demonstrate care. It's not the difficulty of the topic but the manner in which it is addressed that determines the relational outcome. Modeling vulnerability is one of the most courageous relational acts a leader can take. Sharing personal challenges, professional setbacks, or ongoing learning efforts shows that leadership is a journey.

Vulnerability removes the façade of perfection and makes space for authentic connection. Ultimately, relationship-building in leadership is about building legacy. Long after metrics fade, people will remember how a leader made them feel, how they were treated, and whether they felt a sense of belonging. Great leaders are not just remembered for what they accomplished but for how they nurtured the people around them. When relationships are prioritized in leadership, team members are more likely to advocate for one another and operate from a mindset of collective responsibility.

This shared accountability leads to stronger team dynamics, as everyone feels responsible for both individual and group success. Recognition that is tailored to individual preferences strengthens relationships more than one-size-fits-all acknowledgments. Some team members may value public praise, while others prefer private recognition or a simple thank-you note. Personalized recognition signals that leaders see people as individuals, not just roles. Cross-cultural relationship-building also enhances global collaboration.

As organizations grow and connect across borders, leaders must develop cultural agility—the ability to communicate and build trust across cultural norms, languages, and expectations. Cultural agility fosters international harmony and opens doors for innovation. The use of positive language contributes to healthier relational climates. Leaders who speak with optimism, encouragement, and clarity help shape a culture where people feel supported. Words matter, and consistent positive language reinforces relational trust and emotional well-being.

Relationships also thrive when leaders focus on shared meaning. Aligning team efforts with a common vision or higher purpose cultivates unity and motivation. When individuals see how their contributions connect to a bigger mission, they feel more invested and collaborative. Digital empathy is an emerging skill as virtual communication becomes standard. Leaders must be mindful of tone in emails, the frequency of check-ins, and the importance of non-verbal cues in video calls.

Empathy expressed through digital platforms reinforces relationships even when face-to-face interaction is limited. Leaders who embrace feedback with gratitude model humility. When they listen to input from team members and acknowledge insights without defensiveness, they encourage open dialogue. This dynamic enhances relational trust and helps shape more responsive, inclusive leadership practices. Relationship-oriented leaders are future-focused in their development of people.

They don't just mentor for current performance—they guide for future potential. This proactive development signals belief in others and cultivates long-term loyalty and growth. When leaders forgive minor mistakes, it sets a tone of grace and maturity. Forgiveness, when coupled with accountability, prevents grudges and resentment from taking root. It reinforces the idea that relationships can withstand conflict and evolve through honest dialogue.

Finally, relationships are the connective tissue of leadership. They turn ideas into movements, policies into cultures, and teams into families. The leaders who invest consistently in relationships leave behind more than just programs—they leave behind empowered people who carry the mission forward. Leaders must also learn the art of relational timing. Knowing when to push, when to pause, and when to listen is a skill refined through relational attentiveness.

Some of the most powerful leadership decisions are made not by action, but by patience in the presence of another's need. Sustained relationships also create intergenerational wisdom. Leaders who engage with both younger and older colleagues create bridges between innovation and tradition. This continuity ensures that organizations not only grow but do so in ways that honor the past while embracing the future. Healing is a relational act that leaders often overlook.

When harm has occurred—whether intentional or not—addressing it head-on through listening, apology, and change demonstrates relational maturity. Healing allows individuals and teams to move forward together, stronger and more united. Rituals of reconnection—such as retreats, offsite gatherings, or even shared meals—help to reset and refresh relationships. They offer space for storytelling, celebration, and shared dreaming. These moments can reignite a team's collective spirit and foster deeper cohesion.

In highly competitive environments, leaders who remain relational create safe harbors for their teams. They protect their people from toxic cultures and instead model collaboration over comparison. This kind of leadership shields mental health and preserves dignity in high-pressure situations. Clarity in communication is another relational necessity. Confusion breeds frustration, and frustration can erode trust.

Leaders who communicate with clarity and intention reduce relational friction and promote smoother, more respectful collaboration across teams. Curiosity is a powerful relational tool. Asking thoughtful questions, showing interest in others' backgrounds, and seeking to understand different perspectives all signal that people matter. Curiosity fosters mutual discovery, which deepens connection beyond surface-level interaction. Affirming identity in all forms—cultural, professional, personal—strengthens relationships by signaling acceptance.

Leaders who honor identity create inclusive spaces where everyone feels valued for who they are, not just what they do. These affirmations promote belonging at every level. Even endings can be relational. How a leader exits a role or supports someone transitioning out of a team shapes lasting perceptions. Departures done with grace, gratitude, and closure preserve trust and extend relationships beyond formal roles or titles.

At its heart, leadership through relationships is about cultivating human dignity. It is the practice of saying, again and again, through words and actions: You matter. We belong. We are in this together. And when that message is lived consistently, it leaves a legacy that endures far beyond the leader's tenure.

Relational leadership also demands consistency. Inconsistency in tone, attention, or follow-through can weaken the relational fabric leaders work so hard to build. Consistent behavior, grounded in values, helps others feel secure and confident in their interactions, which in turn builds loyalty and long-term trust. Mentorship is one of the most powerful vehicles for relational influence. A strong mentor doesn't just pass on knowledge; they invest emotionally, walk alongside, and cheer from the sidelines.

The long-term nature of mentorship demonstrates a leader's commitment to another person's journey—not just their results. When relationships are seen as strategic assets and not soft skills, leadership becomes transformational. Organizations that emphasize relationship-based leadership outperform others not only in morale but also in innovation, retention, and resilience. The most future-ready workplaces will be those that invest in relationships today.

Chapter 6: Resilience and Recovery

Resilience is not merely the ability to withstand pressure; it is the capacity to recover, to learn, and to grow through adversity. In leadership, resilience acts as a cornerstone of long-term effectiveness. It equips leaders to endure challenges without losing vision or direction, and it models perseverance for those they serve. Recovery, often overlooked in leadership discourse, is equally important. It is in recovery that we process our experiences, restore our strength, and recalibrate our priorities.

Leaders who build rhythms of recovery into their lives sustain their performance and their impact far beyond those who do not. True resilience begins with mindset. Leaders who frame adversity as an opportunity for refinement rather than as a threat to their status or success are more likely to rebound. This growth-oriented perspective doesn't deny pain but instead finds meaning within it. Resilient leaders cultivate self-awareness.

They know their limits and recognize early signs of burnout, stress, or emotional fatigue. Self-awareness allows them to take proactive measures before reaching a breaking point, demonstrating responsibility not only to themselves but also to those they lead. One of the most powerful tools in recovery is rest. Rest is not a sign of weakness but a strategy for strength. Leaders who normalize rest—mental, physical, emotional, and spiritual—create space for innovation, clarity, and renewed energy.

Support systems are essential to both resilience and recovery. Mentors, peer networks, family, and faith communities all serve as pillars that uphold leaders during turbulent seasons. Strong relationships offer perspective and remind leaders that they are not alone in their journey. Resilience is reinforced through reflection. Taking time to assess what went wrong, what was learned, and what will be done differently next time helps transform setbacks into stepping stones.

Reflection turns pain into wisdom and loss into leadership. Adaptability is a key attribute of resilient leadership. The ability to adjust course in response to new data, shifting priorities, or unforeseen obstacles ensures that leaders remain relevant and effective. Flexibility is not indecision—it is strategic responsiveness. Leaders must model emotional regulation in times of crisis.

This doesn't mean suppressing emotion but managing it in a way that provides stability for the team. A calm, steady presence can inspire confidence even when circumstances are uncertain. Narrative reconstruction is a powerful recovery technique. By reinterpreting experiences through a lens of purpose and progress, leaders regain agency over their story. They no longer see themselves as victims of circumstances but as stewards of transformation.

A key component of resilience is intentional preparation. Leaders who anticipate adversity by building mental, emotional, and organizational reserves are more likely to respond rather than react. Preparation doesn't prevent hardship—it provides the internal scaffolding necessary to navigate it. The ability to bounce forward rather than merely bounce back defines high-impact leadership. Bouncing forward means using hardship as a launchpad to reinvent, reimagine, and rise to new levels of effectiveness.

This orientation transforms struggle into a platform for advancement. Vulnerability plays a critical role in resilience. Leaders who are willing to admit challenges and express authentic emotion create space for others to do the same. Vulnerability builds trust and creates relational safety, both of which are essential for recovery and growth. Resilient leaders remain anchored in purpose.

When circumstances are turbulent, returning to a clear sense of mission brings stability. A strong purpose acts like a compass, guiding leaders through ambiguity and reminding them why the journey is worth the struggle. Stories of past resilience serve as fuel for future challenges. Reflecting on previous wins, recalling moments of perseverance, and revisiting inspirational examples can reignite courage in present adversity. These stories create a mental reservoir leaders can draw from when hope is low.

Recovery also depends on boundary setting. Leaders who guard their time, energy, and mental focus protect the space needed for rest and reflection. Boundaries are not barriers to productivity—they are bridges to sustainability. Mindfulness practices such as journaling, meditation, and breathwork support resilience by centering the mind and body. Leaders who incorporate mindfulness into their routines become more aware of their thoughts, more attuned to their emotions, and more capable of leading with clarity.

Creativity often emerges after crisis. Once the dust settles, leaders who are open to new ways of thinking discover innovative approaches and refreshed vision. Crisis strips away the unnecessary and highlights what truly matters, clearing the path for bold new ideas. Resilience is also cultural. Leaders who foster resilient cultures teach their teams how to respond to failure, celebrate recovery, and pursue learning.

They normalize mistakes as part of growth and equip others to rebound with confidence and courage. The emotional toll of leadership during crisis can be invisible but immense. Leaders must acknowledge their emotional needs and seek counseling, coaching, or confidential peer support when necessary. Emotional resilience is a form of wisdom, not weakness. In environments where failure is punished rather than explored, resilience withers.

Leaders must create psychological safety, where team members feel free to take risks, admit mistakes, and share concerns. This culture allows individuals and groups to recover quickly from setbacks and try again with renewed vigor. Leadership often demands calm in chaos. The ability to maintain composure during moments of high stress not only steadies the team but also models emotional intelligence. Leaders who remain calm under pressure communicate to their teams that challenges are manageable, even when difficult.

Recovery is optimized when it is proactive, not reactive. Leaders should not wait for burnout or breakdown to prioritize well-being. Regularly scheduled breaks, intentional downtime, and mental health practices build a buffer that enables faster and more complete recovery after stress. Community plays a critical role in recovery. Whether it's a close-knit work team or a broader support network, connection with others helps distribute the emotional weight of leadership.

Shared burdens become lighter, and shared encouragement strengthens the will to continue. One of the most underutilized strategies for resilience is gratitude. Practicing gratitude—individually and collectively—shifts focus from what's going wrong to what's still going right. This perspective cultivates optimism, strengthens relationships, and keeps hope alive even in difficulty. Leaders must also practice self-compassion.

The inner critic is often louder in high-performing individuals, and failures can feel deeply personal. However, self-compassion allows leaders to acknowledge their humanity, learn from missteps, and move forward without becoming paralyzed by guilt or shame. Building resilience requires a shift from perfectionism to perseverance. Leaders who let go of the need to always get it right free themselves to grow. Resilience is forged not in flawless execution but in the willingness to continue learning, adapting, and leading despite imperfection.

Recovery is a multilayered process. It includes emotional recovery from conflict, physical recovery from exhaustion, and psychological recovery from disappointment or loss. Leaders who attend to all dimensions of recovery sustain themselves and serve as more holistic role models for their teams. Telling the truth about adversity helps others find the courage to face their own. When leaders share stories of resilience—complete with fear, failure, and eventual triumph—they normalize the struggle and provide a roadmap for others walking similar paths.

Resilience is not something leaders reserve for work. It must extend to every part of life—family, health, community, and spirit. When leaders practice resilience holistically, their leadership becomes more grounded, authentic, and sustainable across all domains. One hallmark of resilient leadership is the ability to pivot with purpose. Rather than rigidly clinging to old strategies, effective leaders embrace change with curiosity and intentionality.

This openness to reinvention allows them to lead their teams through disruption with creativity and confidence. Nature often serves as a metaphor for resilience. Trees bend in the wind but don't break because of their flexibility and deep roots. Similarly, leaders grounded in values and guided by a strong sense of identity can flex in the face of adversity without losing their core integrity. Post-traumatic growth is a concept worth integrating into leadership practices.

It suggests that individuals can not only recover from trauma but actually emerge stronger, wiser, and more compassionate. Leaders who embrace post-traumatic growth focus not only on healing but also on elevating their perspective and purpose. Resilience involves grieving what's lost. Whether it's a failed project, a broken relationship, or a missed opportunity, acknowledging grief is an essential part of recovery. Leaders who allow themselves and others to grieve make room for emotional honesty and deeper healing.

In teaching resilience to others, modeling is more impactful than instruction. Teams learn how to recover not through lectures but through watching their leaders respond with dignity and strength. Consistent modeling of resilience reinforces a culture of courage and calm. Leaders who regularly conduct after-action reviews build organizational resilience. These structured reflections after major events—whether successful or not—highlight what worked, what didn't, and what should change next time.

Such practices cultivate learning and prevent repeated missteps. Healthy coping mechanisms distinguish resilient leaders from reactive ones. Exercise, rest, hobbies, spiritual practices, and creative outlets all contribute to a leader's ability to manage stress constructively. Leaders who care for themselves model the importance of holistic well-being for their teams. Sometimes, resilience is about knowing when to walk away.

Not every battle is worth fighting, and not every season requires the same version of the leader. Wisdom is knowing when perseverance turns into stagnation and having the courage to pivot or release what no longer serves the mission. Building resilience at the organizational level requires clear communication and shared expectations. When teams understand their goals, their roles, and the mechanisms for feedback, they are more agile in response to change. Clarity becomes a resilience multiplier.

Finally, resilient leadership embraces hope. Hope is not wishful thinking—it is a confident expectation that something good can come from adversity. Leaders who hold hope in tension with reality provide a stabilizing force, helping others believe in progress even when it's hard to see. Resilient leaders recognize the power of perspective. How they choose to interpret events often determines their emotional trajectory.

Seeing setbacks as setups for new opportunities empowers leaders to move forward with vision instead of becoming trapped in disappointment. When leaders normalize conversations about mental health, they dismantle stigma and foster resilience in others. By being open about seeking counseling, taking mental health days, or managing anxiety, leaders create a safe culture where others feel encouraged to seek support without shame. Consistency in adversity reinforces stability. When people know what to expect from their leaders—even in crisis—they feel more grounded.

Consistent behaviors such as timely communication, clear decision-making, and emotional steadiness give teams something firm to hold onto in turbulent times. Building team resilience involves training, not just encouragement. Equipping teams with conflict resolution skills, time management strategies, and wellness resources empowers them to handle pressure effectively. Prepared teams are confident teams, and confidence is a product of investment. It's essential to honor the emotional toll of change.

Leaders who rush through transitions without acknowledging the losses involved inadvertently suppress growth. Giving people space to express fears, disappointments, and uncertainty fosters honest dialogue and facilitates smoother transitions. Recovery requires leaders to get reacquainted with joy. After hardship, intentionally pursuing joy—whether through family, hobbies, or celebration—restores balance and signals that life is more than just work. Joy builds emotional resilience by reminding leaders of what makes life meaningful.

Resilience also requires leaders to know their values intimately. In moments of stress, values act as non-negotiable anchors that keep them aligned. Decisions made under pressure become more ethical, clear, and consistent when filtered through well-defined personal and organizational values. Leaders who create rituals of reflection help their teams recover more quickly. Weekly debriefs, gratitude circles, or storytelling sessions help team members process events together.

These rituals create emotional closure, which allows energy to be reinvested in future goals. Taking responsibility without taking on guilt is a subtle but vital distinction in recovery. Leaders must be accountable for decisions and outcomes without internalizing every failure. This balance prevents self-blame from eroding confidence and encourages forward momentum. In recovery seasons, flexibility with expectations is critical.

Leaders must recognize when goals need to be adjusted due to capacity constraints or unexpected disruptions. Adjusting expectations doesn't mean lowering standards—it means responding wisely to reality. Crisis leadership often reveals character. While skills and strategies matter, it is the internal compass—integrity, humility, compassion—that guides resilient leaders through the fog. When everything is uncertain, character becomes the clearest guide.

Resilient leaders do not operate in isolation. They actively seek wise counsel. Whether through peer mentorship, advisory boards, or community elders, they tap into diverse perspectives to gain clarity. This communal discernment leads to more informed and courageous decision-making. Sustainable recovery is built on habits, not just heroic moments.

Daily practices—like journaling, gratitude, and exercise—fortify the inner life of a leader. These rituals form the foundation that holds firm when adversity strikes unexpectedly. Restoration includes more than rest; it involves recalibration. Leaders must step back, assess what they've been carrying, and decide what still aligns with their purpose. Recovery gives leaders permission to let go of what's no longer serving their vision.

In team dynamics, leaders who encourage mutual accountability foster resilience. When everyone feels responsible for both outcomes and well-being, teams move beyond blame and into a shared commitment to rise together. This interdependence becomes a source of strength. Resilience thrives in environments of autonomy and trust. Micromanagement erodes confidence, while trust empowers people to act boldly.

Leaders who trust their teams, especially in challenging times, unlock creative solutions and foster loyalty. Effective leaders embrace 'pause moments.' Strategic pauses before responding, deciding, or reacting allow for greater wisdom and empathy. In fast-paced environments, the ability to pause is a rare and transformative leadership trait. Acknowledging 'invisible wounds' in the workplace also promotes recovery. Emotional scars from workplace trauma, toxic cultures, or unspoken losses must be addressed.

Leaders who provide space for healing conversations demonstrate deep care and courage. A forward-focused mindset is vital during recovery. Leaders who dwell only on what was lost risk stagnation.

Those who ask, 'What's possible now?' shift the emotional tone of their teams and help reframe pain into potential. Finally, resilient leaders build legacies of strength.

They mentor others to be adaptable, emotionally agile, and mission-driven. Their influence ripples far beyond their tenure, leaving behind organizations and individuals equipped to thrive in any storm. In the process of recovery, storytelling can be a profound tool. Leaders who craft meaningful narratives about their trials inspire those they lead to frame their own hardships as part of a larger, empowering story. Storytelling brings cohesion to the chaos and meaning to the mess.

The language leaders use during difficult times matters. Words of hope, honesty, and encouragement help shape an environment where people feel secure even in discomfort. Strategic use of affirming language promotes emotional resilience within teams. Resilient leaders don't just bounce back—they rise up with wisdom. Every crisis brings new insights.

Leaders who document their reflections and systematize lessons learned turn temporary setbacks into permanent knowledge that benefits the whole organization. Community-based resilience expands the leadership lens beyond the workplace. Leaders who are active in their neighborhoods, schools, or faith communities model a broader definition of influence—one that is rooted in shared responsibility and mutual care. Digital resilience is now essential. Leaders must adapt not only emotionally but technologically.

Navigating digital transformation, leading hybrid teams, and preserving culture across screens are modern challenges that require agility and innovative thinking. Resilience also means choosing what not to carry. Emotional decluttering—letting go of guilt, outdated expectations, or unresolved tension—frees up space for creativity and renewed focus. Leaders who declutter emotionally show that it's okay to reset and redefine success. Intentional silence is another overlooked tool for recovery.

Moments of stillness—free from noise, screens, or obliga-tions—can provide clarity, calm, and the inner spaciousness needed to reconnect with purpose. In the face of systemic adversity, collective resilience becomes paramount. Leaders who unify their teams around a common vision, even amid external challenges, create solidarity and strength. This kind of resilience transcends individuals and strength-ens communities. Leaders must be fluent in emotional transitions.

The journey from loss to hope, confusion to clarity, or fatigue to energy requires emotional literacy. By naming these transitions and leading others through them, leaders normalize emotional move-ment as part of organizational life. Ultimately, resilient leadership isn't about eliminating adversity—it's about transforming adversity into agency. Leaders who emerge stronger after a challenge not only restore their own confidence but expand the capacity of their entire team to believe, endure, and evolve. Reflection is the mirror through which resilience is often revealed.

Leaders who engage in honest self-evaluation are better equipped to identify growth areas, celebrate endurance, and map a course for-ward with renewed precision. Reflection brings awareness to inner shifts that may otherwise go unnoticed. Time perspective plays a sub-tle but powerful role in recovery. Leaders who keep a long-term view during difficult seasons are more likely to weather temporary discom-fort. This future focus fosters perseverance, reminding them that to-day's challenges are not the final chapter.

Peer empathy fuels collective recovery. When leaders recognize and honor the emotional experiences of their colleagues, it validates struggle and nurtures resilience. Simple gestures—checking in, offer-ing encouragement, or acknowledging contributions—strengthen re-lational bonds and emotional reserves. Reframing is a skill resilient leaders master. By changing the lens through which they view failure, they shift from self-blame to self-improvement.

Reframing allows adversity to become a teacher rather than a tormentor. Spiritual grounding often underpins resilient leadership. Whether through prayer, meditation, or faith in a greater purpose, spiritual practices help leaders make sense of suffering, stay anchored in values, and act with compassion—even when the path forward is unclear. Symbolic closure can mark the transition from pain to healing. Whether it's a team ceremony, a letter of reflection, or a symbolic act of letting go, closure rituals help leaders and their teams move from surviving to thriving with intention and grace.

Resilience is both personal and cultural. Organizations must embed it into their leadership pipelines, onboarding processes, and performance frameworks. When resilience is part of institutional DNA, it becomes less dependent on individuals and more reflective of the organization's ethos. Leaders who practice compassionate accountability accelerate recovery. Holding people to standards while understanding their humanity invites both high performance and high trust.

Compassion fuels sustainable effort and encourages open dialogue during challenging times. Innovation can be a surprising byproduct of adversity. When systems break down, leaders are forced to think differently. Those who remain agile and open to experimentation often discover better methods, deeper truths, and unexpected efficiencies. Finally, resilient leadership must be celebrated.

Recognizing not just the end results but the journey—the grit, the vulnerability, and the persistence—reinforces a culture that values the whole human experience and inspires others to rise through their own storms. The journey of resilience is deeply intertwined with emotional intelligence. Leaders who are self-aware and capable of managing their emotions navigate crises more effectively. Emotional intelligence enables them to recognize distress signals early, regulate their reactions, and extend empathy to others under stress. Mentorship accelerates resilience by offering leaders a sounding board and source of wisdom.

A trusted mentor can offer perspective during turmoil and share lessons from their own path of perseverance. This relational support system builds courage in the face of adversity. Burnout prevention is not a luxury—it is a leadership imperative. Leaders who push through without pause often crash without warning. Recognizing early signs of fatigue, delegating responsibilities, and prioritizing recovery allow leaders to preserve their effectiveness for the long haul.

Transparency during hard times builds organizational trust. When leaders openly communicate setbacks, shifts in plans, or challenges ahead, it cultivates collective ownership. People are more resilient when they feel informed and included, not shielded or surprised. Systemic resilience calls for structural flexibility. Rigid protocols may falter under pressure, but systems that allow for adaptability support sustained recovery.

Leaders must design workflows, communication paths, and timelines that can flex in times of crisis without breaking down. Narrative ownership is a critical aspect of personal recovery. Leaders who craft their own interpretation of events—rather than passively absorbing others' stories—reclaim their power. This ownership fuels confidence, reorients identity, and reinforces a forward-looking posture. Resilient leaders are often skilled at reframing their timelines.

Not everything has to be resolved immediately. By pacing recovery and setting realistic milestones, they avoid emotional whiplash and build stamina for sustained transformation. The discipline of solitude is essential in leadership resilience. Solitude is where leaders clarify intentions, confront fears, and generate creative solutions away from external noise. Carving out space for uninterrupted thought fosters depth and insight.

Recovery also includes strategic re-engagement. After stepping back, leaders must choose when and how to re-enter the arena. Doing so with intentionality ensures that they don't return simply out of habit, but with renewed strength, vision, and direction. Ultimately, resilient leadership is not just about surviving the storm—it's about emerging with greater clarity, compassion, and conviction. The storms may shape the leader, but it is the leader's response that defines the legacy.

Adversity often reveals untapped dimensions of leadership. Resilient leaders recognize that crisis is not just a test but also a mirror, reflecting back their blind spots and hidden strengths. What they learn in the depths of disruption becomes the blueprint for future growth. Celebrating small wins is vital to maintaining morale during recovery. Leaders who acknowledge incremental progress help reframe the narrative from 'what's still wrong' to 'what's already improving.' These moments create momentum and encourage sustained effort.

Leaders must also master the art of emotional pacing. Just as physical recovery requires rest days, emotional recovery requires downtime from high-stakes decisions. Leaders who respect the rhythm of healing are more likely to maintain long-term effectiveness. Cross-training within teams enhances collective resilience. When people are equipped to take on multiple roles, organizations become less vulnerable to disruption.

Cross-functional skills ensure that no single point of failure can derail progress. Courageous conversations are cornerstones of resilient cultures. Leaders who confront hard truths with honesty, respect, and empathy help teams process pain, realign goals, and rebuild trust. Avoiding these conversations often delays or derails recovery. Investing in the next generation of leaders is a resilient act.

Succession planning and mentorship cultivate a legacy of strength. When leadership is distributed, organizations thrive even when top leaders are absent or transitioning. Flexibility in leadership style fosters resilience. Situational leadership—adjusting one's approach based on the context and people involved—helps teams feel supported and understood. Rigid leadership styles often crack under pressure, while adaptive ones endure.

The stories we tell ourselves shape our resilience. Internal narratives of strength, growth, and learning build psychological endurance. Leaders who reshape self-talk from criticism to compassion shift their mindset from defeat to determination. Resilient organizations build in redundancy not out of pessimism, but out of foresight. Backup systems, contingency plans, and flexible staffing models ensure stability.

Anticipating obstacles and preparing solutions is not weakness—it's strategic wisdom. Ultimately, resilient leaders are hope carriers. Even in the darkest moments, they hold the torch of possibility. Their steady presence offers reassurance that the storm will pass—and that when it does, a stronger, wiser version of the team will emerge. Self-renewal is a cornerstone of resilience.

Leaders who prioritize personal renewal—through retreat, reflection, or recreation—prevent burnout and enhance their creativity. These cycles of intentional withdrawal and return promote longevity in leadership. Resilient leaders create a culture of feedback, not fear. Open dialogue and constructive criticism ensure that mistakes become learning opportunities, not sources of shame. This environment fosters growth, agility, and shared accountability.

Spiritual intelligence, while often overlooked, provides a deep well of resilience. A sense of higher purpose, inner peace, or moral clarity empowers leaders to remain grounded during upheaval. This internal compass guides behavior when external conditions are unstable. Adaptability extends to emotions as much as plans. Leaders who stay emotionally agile—able to shift from grief to gratitude, frustration to focus—create emotional balance for themselves and those they lead.

This flexibility reduces reactivity and promotes poise. The concept of antifragility elevates resilience. Coined by Nassim Nicholas Taleb, antifragility describes systems that grow stronger through volatility. Leaders who embrace disruption as fuel for development move beyond recovery to renewal and reinvention. Generosity is a recovery catalyst.

When leaders offer time, support, or recognition to others during difficult seasons, they shift focus from scarcity to abundance. This giving spirit builds goodwill and replenishes emotional reserves on both sides. Humor can be a powerful antidote to despair. Leaders who can laugh—appropriately and authentically—even in difficulty, model emotional resilience. Humor disarms fear, invites connection, and humanizes leadership in profound ways.

Clarity amid chaos builds resilience across teams. When leaders articulate what remains unchanged—the mission, the values, the community bond—it provides psychological safety. Anchoring to these constants helps navigate ambiguity with confidence. Resilient leaders also manage their digital diet. Overconsumption of bad news, comparison, and crisis can erode well-being.

By curating their media intake and prioritizing real connection, leaders protect their energy and maintain mental clarity. The ripple effects of resilience are generational. Leaders who model grace under pressure, values-based decisions, and emotional transparency leave behind not just a stronger organization, but a blueprint for those who follow. Their legacy becomes a map for others to navigate difficulty with courage and hope. Forgiveness plays a silent but powerful role in recovery.

Leaders who forgive themselves for missteps and others for failings foster emotional release. This act of grace dismantles resentment, making space for renewed trust and forward movement. The ability to compartmentalize, when used wisely, supports resilience. It allows leaders to temporarily set aside emotionally heavy matters in order to focus on immediate needs. When balanced with intentional processing, compartmentalization prevents emotional overload.

Team rituals that mark resilience can build unity. Whether through shared meals, reflection sessions, or symbolic celebrations, these collective practices remind everyone that they have endured something meaningful together—and are stronger because of it. Boundary-setting is another skill that strengthens recovery. Leaders must distinguish between helpful availability and unhealthy overextension. Protecting their time, energy, and mental space ensures they can lead with clarity and sustain their influence.

Resilient recovery demands clarity of purpose. When leaders realign with their personal and organizational 'why,' they regain energy and momentum. Purpose clarifies priorities, informs decisions, and infuses meaning into even the most difficult circumstances. Gratitude practices build emotional immunity. When leaders consciously identify what is still good, stable, or worthy of celebration—even in hardship—they train their minds to notice abundance.

This shift in awareness fosters optimism and balance. Building resilience includes embracing imperfection. Leaders who accept that mistakes, failures, and detours are part of the leadership journey reduce self-judgment and increase emotional freedom. This mindset encourages innovation and courageous decision-making. Nature offers inspiration for resilient leadership.

Observing how ecosystems recover after storms, how trees grow through concrete, and how animals adapt to changing conditions reminds leaders that resilience is a universal law—one that they, too, can embody. Listening deeply is an underrated recovery tool. Leaders who listen without interruption, with full presence, create healing space. Listening validates experience, diffuses tension, and reinforces the human connection so vital to organizational healing. Ultimately, the essence of resilience lies in the return.

Not just returning to work, but returning to purpose, passion, and presence. Leaders who walk back into their mission with a renewed sense of clarity and compassion become not only survivors but also stewards of renewal. Resilience is enhanced when leaders embrace a posture of learning rather than control. Letting go of the need to have all the answers invites humility, curiosity, and a willingness to adapt—three qualities essential for sustainable growth during adversity. Leaders who invest in post-crisis reflection sessions with their teams not only process the event together but harvest wisdom from the experience.

These sessions create space for shared meaning-making and build stronger alignment moving forward. Cultural rituals—such as storytelling, honoring milestones, or collective silence—reinforce organizational memory. They remind teams of what they overcame and who they became in the process, fostering identity and unity rooted in resilience. Resilient leadership includes anticipating the next wave. Once recovery is underway, wise leaders begin preparing for future challenges by strengthening infrastructure, building capacity, and documenting lessons learned.

Preparedness is the quiet partner of resilience. Collaboration across departments or sectors often accelerates recovery. Leaders who foster interdependence and cross-functional teamwork discover innovative solutions that may not arise in silos. Resilience is not just personal—it's relational and systemic. Leaders who document their recovery journey contribute to the broader leadership field.

By writing, speaking, or mentoring about what they endured and learned, they inspire others and preserve insights that can serve as guideposts in future storms. Resilience in leadership doesn't demand perfection—it demands presence. Showing up authentically, engaging with integrity, and continuing the mission, even while healing, sends a powerful message that strength and vulnerability can coexist. As recovery reaches maturity, celebration becomes essential. Leaders who acknowledge how far they and their teams have come reinforce a sense of accomplishment.

These celebrations do not erase pain—they honor perseverance and recognize progress. Leaders committed to resilience ensure that recovery is not episodic but embedded. They create policies, rhythms, and expectations that support wellbeing at every level. This culture of resilience becomes a permanent feature, not a temporary fix. The final note of resilient leadership is hope.

Not blind optimism, but grounded, persistent belief in what is possible. Leaders who embody hope amid hardship become beacons—guiding their teams not only to bounce back, but to rise stronger than before.

Chapter 7: Vision, Voice, and Values

Vision is the cornerstone of all meaningful leadership. Without a clear picture of where an organization or community is headed, even the most talented teams can drift.

A leader's vision serves as the north star—providing direction, inspiring commitment, and anchoring the collective purpose. Strategic planning gives the vision legs. It takes the abstract and turns it into actionable steps, measurable goals, and sustainable processes. While vision is emotional and expansive, strategy is precise and practical. Together, they form the heartbeat of successful leadership.

Effective vision casting begins with listening. Great leaders don't impose a vision—they uncover it. Through dialogue with stakeholders, reflection on core values, and analysis of present realities, they shape a vision that resonates across roles and reaches beyond individual ambition. A compelling vision must be communicated clearly and consistently. Repetition reinforces belief.

Leaders who integrate vision into meetings, emails, onboarding, and daily interactions ensure that it becomes more than a statement—it becomes a culture. Leaders must paint the vision vividly. Storytelling, metaphors, and imagery help people feel the future before it arrives. When individuals can see themselves in the vision, they are more likely to commit their energy and talents to achieving it. Strategic planning is most effective when it includes diverse voices.

Teams that incorporate feedback from across departments, roles, and even community partners design more holistic strategies. Inclusion leads to innovation and fosters greater buy-in. Clear objectives are the backbone of a strategic plan. Goals should be SMART: Specific, Measurable, Achievable, Relevant, and Time-bound. These guideposts allow teams to monitor progress and adjust course when necessary, without losing momentum.

Data informs sound planning. Leaders who utilize performance metrics, environmental scans, and trend analyses make informed decisions. While intuition has its place, data-driven planning creates credibility and clarity around what is possible and what must change. Strategic leaders break vision into phases. They recognize that transformation takes time and that quick wins build trust.

By outlining short-, medium-, and long-term milestones, leaders can sustain enthusiasm and demonstrate steady progress. Accountability structures are essential for strategic follow-through. Regular check-ins, transparent reporting, and feedback loops ensure that vision does not stagnate in planning documents. Execution is the true measure of strategic effectiveness. Strategic alignment is the bridge between daily operations and long-term vision.

Leaders who ensure that every team member understands how their role contributes to the broader strategy create a sense of ownership and motivation. Alignment turns isolated effort into collective momentum. The most resilient strategies are adaptable. Vision may remain constant, but the path to realizing it often shifts. Strategic leaders build in flexibility, preparing for multiple scenarios and empowering teams to pivot without losing purpose.

Resource allocation is a strategic decision, not a logistical task. Where a leader places time, money, and personnel signals what matters most. Prioritizing resources in alignment with vision demonstrates integrity and fuels consistent progress. Stakeholder engagement is a critical element of strategic planning. Leaders who invite partners, funders, community members, and even critics into the planning process build stronger relationships and more durable plans.

Shared strategy creates shared investment. Strategic foresight is a leader's ability to anticipate emerging trends and respond proactively. Whether navigating technological change, demographic shifts, or policy updates, foresight allows organizations to act with intention rather than react out of urgency. Leaders must build systems for feedback and iteration. Strategy is not a static blueprint—it's a living framework.

Regular reviews, open dialogue, and transparent reporting keep the strategy relevant and responsive to new information. Training and capacity-building are vital for execution. It is not enough to have a good plan—teams must be equipped to carry it out. Leaders who invest in development ensure that their people can deliver at every stage of the vision. Leaders must also guard against 'strategic drift,' where daily pressures pull teams away from long-term goals.

By consistently realigning priorities with vision, leaders prevent mission dilution and maintain strategic clarity. Story-driven strategy captures hearts as well as minds. When planning includes personal narratives, shared values, and collective aspirations, it becomes emotionally compelling. Emotional resonance increases commitment, creativity, and resilience. Ultimately, strategic planning is not about predicting the future perfectly—it's about preparing wisely.

Leaders who build thoughtful, inclusive, and flexible plans inspire confidence. They signal to their teams and communities: we are ready, we are capable, and we are moving forward together. Vision, voice, and values form the leadership triad that grounds influence in authenticity and impact. These three components are interwoven threads in the fabric of transformational leadership, allowing individuals to lead with clarity, conviction, and character. A compelling vision is the ability to see beyond the present into a future that inspires action.

Visionary leaders not only imagine better outcomes—they communicate them in ways that others can internalize and pursue. Vision serves as a compass in times of uncertainty and a rallying cry in times of growth. Voice is the unique expression of leadership. It includes how a leader communicates, advocates, and represents their beliefs. Leaders with a powerful voice do not merely speak—they resonate.

Their words carry weight because they reflect a consistent inner truth and serve the greater good. Values are the non-negotiable principles that define a leader's integrity. They serve as filters for decision-making and behaviors, ensuring that power is exercised ethically. When leaders live their values publicly, they cultivate trust and model moral courage. Aligning vision, voice, and values transforms leadership from positional authority to purposeful influence.

It fosters authenticity, which in turn strengthens the emotional bond between leaders and those they serve. Authentic leadership inspires loyalty and long-term commitment. To develop a compelling vision, leaders must begin with reflective clarity. What do they believe is possible? What does success look like in human terms?

Effective visioning requires imagination rooted in purpose, not just productivity or profit. Voice is cultivated through experience and intentional self-awareness. Leaders must examine their personal narratives, cultural identities, and communication styles to identify what gives their voice power. Authenticity is not about volume—it's about resonance. Leaders must regularly examine and articulate their core values.

These values are not just abstract beliefs but lived expressions. When values are consistently applied across diverse situations, they build credibility and demonstrate character under pressure. In diverse and dynamic environments, vision must be adaptable without losing its core essence. Leaders who invite others into the visioning process ensure that the future reflects collective aspirations, not just personal ambition. Values-driven leadership demands courage.

It requires choosing what is right over what is easy or popular. Leaders who stand firm in their values during ethical dilemmas or social pressure build organizational cultures rooted in integrity and resilience. When vision, voice, and values align, they create a leadership brand that is instantly recognizable and profoundly impactful. People know what to expect, trust the consistency, and are more willing to invest in the leader's goals. A leader's voice does not emerge in isolation.

It is shaped by mentors, life experiences, and moments of adversity. The most powerful voices are often forged in silence, through reflection, struggle, and perseverance. This depth gives their words authenticity and power. In times of crisis, values become non-negotiables. They anchor decision-making when the pressure to compromise intensifies.

Leaders who act in alignment with their values—even at personal or professional cost—demonstrate moral courage and build lasting trust. Vision must be revisited regularly. As teams evolve and the environment changes, the vision must stay relevant. Leaders who revisit and revise their vision ensure it remains a living force—not just a framed statement on the wall. The voice of a leader becomes amplified when it reflects the voice of the people.

Great leaders are not just eloquent—they are deeply empathetic. They listen intentionally, speak inclusively, and give voice to those who have been marginalized. Living one's values openly strengthens organizational culture. It encourages others to bring their full selves to the workplace and cultivates a sense of safety. In value-driven cultures, people are more willing to take risks, speak honestly, and collaborate authentically.

Vision should stretch the imagination while remaining grounded in the possible. A visionary leader inspires others by connecting today's actions to tomorrow's outcomes. They paint a picture of the future that is both inspiring and attainable. Voice also includes how a leader responds to challenge. Silence in moments that demand speaking up can damage credibility.

Leaders must use their voice to defend justice, promote equity, and champion their values in public arenas—not just private reflections. Values-driven leadership builds legacy. While accomplishments may fade, the impact of a values-based leader endures in the people they shaped, the culture they nurtured, and the example they set. Their influence ripples beyond their tenure. In the final analysis, vision gives purpose, voice gives expression, and values give integrity.

Leaders who cultivate all three lead not just with power, but with purpose. They do not simply direct change—they embody it. True vision transcends personal gain. It is oriented toward collective advancement, grounded in service, and rooted in justice. Leaders with selfless vision inspire movements, not just moments, because they tap into the human desire to be part of something greater.

A refined voice is both bold and measured. Bold enough to speak truth with courage, yet measured enough to maintain humility. Effective leaders know when to speak, when to listen, and when to amplify other voices that need to be heard. Values become particularly visible in conflict. It is easy to preach integrity when times are calm, but under stress, one's true principles are revealed.

Leaders must demonstrate through action that values are not situational—they are foundational. Vision must also be emotionally engaging. Beyond logic and planning, a compelling vision stirs hearts. When people are emotionally invested in a future outcome, they commit their full energy and creativity to bring it into reality. Voice is a leadership instrument.

Like any instrument, it must be practiced, refined, and tuned to context. Great leaders adapt their tone, language, and style without compromising truth. They communicate with empathy, urgency, and clarity. In values-driven organizations, ethical decision-making is a shared responsibility. Everyone is encouraged to hold one another accountable.

This shared moral compass reduces ambiguity and increases alignment across teams and departments. Strategic visioning involves scanning both internal dynamics and external trends. Leaders who understand their environment are more effective at identifying opportunities and threats, and they craft visions that are both aspirational and realistic. Voice also shapes culture. The language leaders use sets the tone for dialogue, relationships, and conflict resolution.

Leaders who speak with respect and inclusivity create cultures that mirror those values in every interaction. Values should be visible in policies and practices—not just posters and slogans. When hiring, promotions, and evaluations reflect stated values, the organization reinforces a culture of accountability and integrity. The intersection of vision, voice, and values defines legacy. Leaders who intentionally develop these areas leave behind more than results—they leave behind a model of leadership that others can follow, adapt, and honor for generations.

Vision, voice, and values serve as leadership infrastructure. Without these foundational elements, any organizational initiative may lack direction, cohesion, and purpose. Together, they form a framework for leading with clarity and consistency. When a leader's voice carries empathy and empowerment, it can reframe setbacks as opportunities. The language of possibility turns obstacles into stepping stones.

It reminds teams that challenges do not define them—resilience does. Vision should be aspirational but actionable. A lofty vision that cannot be translated into steps risks becoming rhetoric. Effective leaders break their vision into attainable goals, allowing individuals to track their contribution to a broader impact. Voice is also about advocacy.

Leaders must speak up for those who cannot. Whether it's championing underserved communities, addressing inequities, or challenging the status quo, a strong leadership voice disrupts complacency and calls for justice. Values-based leadership creates continuity. Even during leadership transitions, a clear and embedded set of values ensures that the organization's soul remains intact. Values serve as institutional memory and a compass for new leaders.

Leaders must periodically revisit their values to ensure they still reflect their beliefs and aspirations. Life experience, shifting societal dynamics, and deepened self-awareness may lead to refining or reaffirming core values. Vision, when developed collaboratively, fosters collective ownership. When stakeholders see their input reflected in the vision, they feel seen and valued. Ownership translates to higher engagement and deeper commitment.

Voice also plays a role in shaping systems. Leaders who use their voice to influence policy, challenge unjust practices, or amplify marginalized perspectives reshape institutional norms. Their voice becomes a catalyst for transformation. To lead with values requires consistency in both private and public settings. It's not only about grand gestures of principle but about daily decisions, ethical consistency, and the discipline to stay grounded when no one is watching.

In times of volatility, vision provides hope, voice provides direction, and values provide steadiness. Together, they anchor people in purpose, navigate them through complexity, and build cultures resilient enough to grow through disruption. Vision, voice, and values do not exist in silos. They overlap, reinforce one another, and together create a cohesive leadership identity. Leaders who embrace this integration lead with alignment—what they say, do, and believe are in harmony.

Voice is not merely about communication—it's about presence. How a leader shows up in a room, listens in meetings, and responds under pressure speaks volumes. A silent leader with a strong presence often influences more than a loud one lacking substance. A vision grounded in shared values becomes a moral imperative. It invites others to commit not because they are obligated, but because they believe.

That kind of commitment fuels sustainable action that outlasts any singular initiative. Leaders must mentor others in finding their voice. Empowering emerging leaders to express their ideas, advocate for their beliefs, and stand confidently in their perspectives builds organizational depth and succession readiness. Values offer stability in uncertainty. In fast-changing environments, values help filter the noise.

Leaders who stay grounded in values can pivot strategies without compromising their core identity. Vision casting should be a continual process. Rather than a one-time announcement, it becomes an evolving dialogue. Leaders who continually revisit and refresh their vision in response to shifting realities model flexibility and foresight. Voice includes knowing when to be quiet.

There is strength in silence, especially when it creates space for others to speak. Leaders who listen actively send the message that everyone's voice matters, not just their own. Values-driven organizations are often more innovative. When people feel safe to bring their full selves to work—knowing that integrity and purpose are valued—they are more creative, risk-tolerant, and mission-aligned. Vision gives organizations their 'why,' values their 'how,' and voice their 'what.' This trifecta ensures that every action is intentional, every message is meaningful, and every goal is rooted in principle.

When vision, voice, and values become cultural norms—not just leadership traits—they cascade throughout the organization. Teams align, communities trust, and momentum builds from a foundation of integrity and shared aspiration. Leaders who ground their leadership in vision, voice, and values create ecosystems of trust. This trust is not earned overnight but cultivated through consistency, transparency, and the genuine care leaders extend to those they serve. A compelling vision doesn't just inspire action—it instills hope.

Especially in challenging seasons, a clearly communicated vision provides a psychological anchor, reminding individuals and teams that their work is meaningful and their future is worth pursuing. Voice is not just a leadership tool; it's a leadership responsibility. When leaders fail to use their voice to advocate for justice, fairness, or team well-being, they relinquish an opportunity to influence change where it is most needed. Values make leaders relatable. When individuals see their leader grappling with ethical choices, acknowledging mistakes, and making decisions aligned with values, it humanizes leadership.

Vulnerability strengthens credibility when grounded in integrity. The development of vision, voice, and values requires intentional reflection. Leaders must build in time for solitude, strategic dialogue, and feedback loops to ensure these elements are not only well-defined but actively evolving with context. Shared vision strengthens collaboration. When a team shares ownership of a vision, collaboration flows more naturally.

Silos dissolve, and people become more willing to contribute their best ideas and challenge the status quo for the greater good. A clear leadership voice shapes institutional identity. Whether in education, nonprofit, or corporate environments, the language and messaging of leadership influences how the entire organization presents itself internally and externally. Living out values also means modeling difficult conversations. Avoiding conflict erodes trust, while addressing issues transparently and respectfully reinforces a culture of accountability.

Values aren't just about kindness—they're about courage. Vision should be visually accessible. Leaders who use metaphors, imagery, and storytelling make the vision tangible and memorable. A story-anchored vision leaves an emotional imprint that outlasts bullet points and spreadsheets. Voice, when rooted in humility, invites collaboration.

Leaders who speak from a place of shared purpose rather than personal ego empower others to contribute meaningfully, creating cultures where leadership is distributed, not hoarded. Organizations that thrive over the long term are those whose leaders build a strong culture grounded in vision, voice, and values. These principles guide behavior and shape identity long after the leader has moved on. A shared vision fosters a sense of belonging. People are more committed when they see their role contributing to something bigger than themselves.

This sense of alignment increases productivity, motivation, and loyalty. Voice is critical during change. Transitions and transformations often spark fear and confusion. A leader who communicates transparently, confidently, and compassionately can stabilize morale and move people from resistance to resilience. Values prevent mission drift.

In fast-paced environments, it's easy for organizations to chase trends or succumb to pressures that stray from their core purpose.

Clearly defined and upheld values help leaders stay grounded amid change. Great leaders teach others how to lead with vision, voice, and values. They create opportunities for reflection, coaching, and real-world application. Leadership development becomes a ripple effect that strengthens the whole community.

Vision is not static; it should grow as the leader grows. As leaders gain new insights, face new challenges, and listen to new voices, their vision should expand to reflect greater wisdom and wider perspectives. Voice should be inclusive. It should reflect the diversity of the people the leader serves. Inclusive leaders use language that honors all identities and communicates with cultural competence and emotional intelligence.

Values should be embedded in decision-making structures. This includes how meetings are conducted, how conflict is resolved, and how success is defined. When values are operationalized, they become tangible and observable. A leader's legacy is often defined not by their accolades but by how faithfully they lived their vision, honored their voice, and upheld their values. This legacy becomes a blueprint for future generations to follow and refine.

Ultimately, vision, voice, and values represent the internal compass of leadership. When aligned, they create a magnetic force that draws people toward excellence, connection, and purpose-driven change. A leader's ability to consistently articulate and act on their vision strengthens alignment throughout an organization. When everyone is working toward a shared destination, it minimizes confusion and maximizes effectiveness. Voice becomes even more powerful when it echoes the lived experiences of others.

Leaders who listen deeply can speak directly to the hopes and frustrations of their people, making their message more impactful and authentic. Values influence how leaders show up in everyday interactions. Whether it's how they greet colleagues, handle feedback, or respond to challenges, values-driven behavior becomes the cultural norm others emulate. Effective visionaries are also great storytellers. They weave a narrative that connects past, present, and future—helping others see where the organization has come from, where it is, and where it's going.

Voice is magnified when paired with credibility. A leader who has earned the respect of their team can speak fewer words with more impact. Their consistency and character amplify their message. In value-centric organizations, accountability is not punitive—it's empowering. Holding people to shared values fosters dignity, fairness, and a collective commitment to growth.

Visionary leaders are often deeply curious. They ask bold questions, seek diverse input, and are open to evolving their perspective. This openness enhances their ability to inspire others with inclusive and relevant goals. Voice can also serve as a healing force. In environments shaped by trauma or injustice, a leader's voice can acknowledge pain, validate emotions, and spark renewal through compassionate truth-telling.

Values determine what a leader is willing to sacrifice. Leaders who remain principled even when it costs them popularity, promotions, or perks demonstrate that integrity is not situational but essential. When vision, voice, and values converge, they create an atmosphere of trust, transparency, and transformation. This convergence elevates leadership from positional power to personal and organizational purpose. Visionary leadership is not limited to setting strategic direction; it's about creating meaning.

Leaders help others connect their daily efforts to a greater sense of purpose, reinforcing why their work matters. A powerful voice bridges gaps. It closes the distance between departments, demographics, and differing perspectives. Through thoughtful communication, a leader's voice becomes the thread that weaves unity from diversity. When a leader upholds values, they create predictability in how decisions are made.

This predictability enhances psychological safety, empowering team members to contribute without fear of arbitrary judgment. Vision must also be inclusive. It should account for those who have been historically overlooked or underrepresented. An inclusive vision invites every stakeholder to see themselves as part of the future. Voice is not a solo act; it's a chorus.

The most effective leaders use their platform to elevate the voices of others. This shared leadership strengthens community, builds trust, and multiplies impact. Values-driven leaders often find clarity in conflict. They don't shy away from tough decisions, but instead use their values as a compass. Even when outcomes are unpopular, their integrity preserves respect.

Leadership vision is sustained by optimism. Hope fuels resilience, and leaders who remain hopeful even in difficult times become beacons of strength for those around them. A cultivated voice adapts to different audiences. Leaders who understand their audience—whether students, board members, or community stakeholders—can communicate with both relevance and resonance. Values should be interwoven into recognition and reward systems.

When teams see values reflected in what is celebrated, they understand what truly matters and align their behaviors accordingly. Ultimately, when leaders consistently model vision, voice, and values, they don't just influence performance—they influence people. They nurture belief, develop capacity, and leave a legacy of empowered individuals prepared to lead the next generation. Vision provides a rallying point for people across roles, ranks, and regions. It becomes the unifying statement that galvanizes collective energy and offers clarity when complexity threatens to divide.

Leaders refine their voice over time. Through feedback, experience, and intentional growth, a leader's voice becomes more authentic and impactful. It gains depth, authority, and influence through lived experience. Values must be reinforced through systems and structures. If values remain philosophical but disconnected from how people are hired, trained, and promoted, they remain aspirational instead of operational.

A visionary leader anticipates not only trends but also needs. They ask: Who is being left behind? What is not being said? What future challenges can we prepare for today? Voice is also deeply connected to emotional intelligence.

Leaders who can name, understand, and regulate emotions communicate more effectively and foster healthier, more transparent organizational cultures. When values are demonstrated from the top, they cascade downward. Staff, students, and stakeholders internalize the culture not from mandates, but from modeling. Leaders set the tone, whether intentionally or not. Vision can be a source of healing.

Communities that have experienced trauma or stagnation often need a renewed vision to restore belief in possibility. A leader's vision can reawaken purpose and promise. Leaders with a seasoned voice know when to speak from the heart, from data, or from collective wisdom. The ability to draw from multiple sources lends their communication power and nuance. Values clarify priorities.

When leaders face competing demands, their values illuminate what matters most. This clarity strengthens decision-making and fosters courage under pressure. At the intersection of vision, voice, and values lies influence. Influence that transcends authority, earns respect, and cultivates transformation. It is this type of influence that leaves a mark on both people and progress.

When leaders share their personal values transparently, they cultivate authenticity and invite others to do the same. This openness nurtures an environment where alignment and belonging thrive. A leader's voice is amplified through storytelling. Stories help people see themselves in the mission and make abstract values come alive through real-world application. The best leaders are often the best storytellers.

Vision invites others to co-create. While a leader may initiate the vision, its refinement and execution benefit from inclusive collaboration. The more voices involved, the more comprehensive and sustainable the outcome. Values-driven decision-making protects long-term outcomes. While expedient shortcuts may be tempting, adherence to values ensures that success is earned with integrity and is more likely to endure.

A clear voice guides organizations through ambiguity. In moments of uncertainty, the leader's tone, clarity, and intentionality can make the difference between chaos and cohesion. Embedding values into evaluation systems ensures that performance is not only measured by results, but by how those results are achieved. It balances excellence with ethics. When a vision is compelling, it mobilizes passion.

People are willing to go above and beyond when they believe they are building something meaningful. Vision energizes effort and commitment. Voice must be courageous. Leaders must speak up even when it is uncomfortable or unpopular. Silence in the face of injustice is complicity.

Leadership voice must be morally bold. Values influence the kind of relationships leaders form. When integrity, respect, and accountability are non-negotiable, leaders attract like-minded collaborators who strengthen the organizational fabric. The ultimate expression of vision, voice, and values is legacy. It's not just what a leader accomplishes during their tenure, but what they leave behind—a culture, a standard, a purpose—that endures after they are gone.

The best leaders revisit their vision with each milestone achieved, using it as both a compass and a checkpoint to ensure progress is still aligned with purpose. A leader's voice can unify diverse teams. Through intentional language and acknowledgment of multiple perspectives, a leader's communication can transcend differences and inspire unity. Values become the invisible hand that shapes culture.

While not always explicitly stated, values show up in how people treat one another, respond to adversity, and celebrate success. Vision turns resistance into resilience. When people understand the 'why' behind change, they are more likely to embrace challenges with resolve rather than fear. Voice, when used intentionally, clarifies priorities. A strong communicator ensures that teams understand not only what needs to be done, but why it matters and how it reflects shared values.

Leaders who ground their voice in empathy create psychological safety. People feel seen, heard, and understood, which fosters collaboration, creativity, and courage. Visionary leaders cast a future that stretches the imagination without losing touch with reality. They balance aspiration with feasibility, helping people believe that great things are not only possible but achievable. Values provide protection from ethical drift.

In moments of pressure or temptation, a well-internalized value system safeguards a leader's integrity and the organization's reputation. A voice that reflects conviction draws people in. Even those who disagree can respect a leader who speaks with clarity, honesty, and consistency. When all three—vision, voice, and values—are synchronized, the result is magnetic leadership. Such leaders attract talent, foster loyalty, and inspire transformation at both individual and systemic levels.

Vision needs storytelling, but it also needs structure. The best leaders support their vision with clear steps, milestones, and accountability mechanisms that convert inspiration into implementation. A powerful voice is consistent, yet adaptive. It remains rooted in core beliefs while adjusting tone and delivery to meet the moment and the audience with relevance and grace. Values are not just aspirational; they are actionable.

They show up in budgets, schedules, agendas, and priorities. If values are not visible in practice, they quickly erode into empty rhetoric. A leader's vision should serve as a mirror and a window—a mirror that reflects internal identity and a window that shows a better future that can be built together. Voice becomes a legacy when it outlives the leader. The most effective leaders build capacity in others to carry forward the message and mission long after they've stepped aside.

When values are deeply embedded in a team, they create an internal compass. Even in the absence of direct leadership, the culture continues to reflect shared ethical principles and expectations. Vision, voice, and values collectively shape a leadership narrative. This narrative tells the story not only of what a leader stands for, but how they've chosen to stand—through action, adversity, and alignment. In educational settings, these three pillars are especially critical.

Students and staff alike look for leaders who offer a clear vision for growth, a voice that uplifts and includes, and values that model integrity and equity. The power of vision, voice, and values is that they transcend context. Whether leading a school, a nonprofit, a business, or a movement, these elements foster sustainable leadership and meaningful impact. When these principles are practiced with courage and consistency, they turn leaders into catalysts—igniting change not just within their organizations, but across communities and generations.

Chapter 8: Empathy in Action

Empathy is often misunderstood as a soft or passive trait, but in leadership, empathy is an active force—a strategic asset that can transform relationships, resolve conflict, and drive results. Empathy in action means moving beyond understanding someone's experience to actually responding in a meaningful and supportive way. In professional settings, empathy builds bridges between people with different perspectives. A leader who takes the time to listen, validate, and acknowledge others' emotions cultivates trust and belonging. These qualities are essential for high-performing teams and resilient organizations.

Empathy requires presence. It demands that leaders slow down enough to fully engage with those they serve. It's about listening not just with ears, but with heart and intention—seeking to understand before seeking to fix. True empathy is not reactive; it's proactive. Empathetic leaders anticipate the needs of others and create structures that support well-being before crises arise.

This kind of foresight builds a culture of care rather than crisis management. Empathy in action shows up in policies and practices. It's seen in flexible work arrangements, mental health initiatives, inclusive hiring, and equitable discipline. When empathy is institutionalized, it creates sustainable change rather than isolated gestures. Empathy also drives innovation.

When teams feel psychologically safe and valued, they are more likely to take creative risks, share ideas, and collaborate freely. Empathy becomes the soil in which innovation grows. In the classroom, empathy manifests in differentiated instruction, restorative practices, and culturally responsive teaching. Educators who lead with empathy see their students not as data points, but as whole people with unique journeys. In communities, empathy is the foundation for social change.

Activists, public servants, and grassroots leaders all rely on empathy to connect with those they advocate for. It fosters solidarity and builds the emotional capital needed to persevere through difficult work. Empathetic leadership is not about being nice; it's about being human. It involves hard conversations, setting boundaries, and making tough decisions with compassion. It's a commitment to seeing the dignity in every person and letting that vision shape every interaction.

Ultimately, empathy in action means creating systems and spaces where people feel safe to be seen, heard, and supported. It transforms organizations from places of performance to places of purpose, where people are not only expected to succeed but equipped to thrive. Empathy is a strategic imperative in leadership, not just a moral one. Leaders who practice empathy create environments where staff engagement and loyalty increase, where turnover declines, and where trust becomes the fabric of the culture. In emotionally intelligent leadership, empathy goes hand in hand with self-awareness.

A leader must first understand and manage their own emotions to effectively tune in to the emotional climate of their teams. Empathy challenges assumptions. It pushes leaders to ask deeper questions, such as: What am I missing? How would I feel in this situation? What does support look like for this person?

Listening with empathy means not just hearing words, but decoding what is unspoken—body language, energy, hesitation, and silence all carry meaning. The empathetic leader leans into these signals with care and curiosity. Empathy is the fuel behind servant leadership. It shifts the power dynamic from command-and-control to support-and-serve. It asks, 'How can I empower you to be your best self in this role?'

The most effective school principals I've known used empathy as a leadership superpower. They didn't just know their students and staff—they understood them. They made decisions that balanced academic expectations with emotional well-being. In community leadership, empathy breaks down barriers of race, class, and culture. It enables coalitions to form across lines of difference, centered on shared humanity and mutual respect.

Empathy doesn't mean avoiding accountability. Rather, it informs how accountability is delivered. A leader can hold high standards and still communicate with grace, fairness, and compassion. Crisis moments often reveal the depth of a leader's empathy. During difficult times, leaders must extend not only strategic guidance but also emotional support, reminding their teams that their humanity is seen and valued.

Empathy in action requires a commitment to equity. It asks leaders to examine systemic injustices and adjust policies, resources, and practices to ensure everyone has access to dignity and opportunity. Leaders who demonstrate empathy are not seen as weak—they are seen as wise. They gain insight into the motivations, challenges, and aspirations of others, making them more effective decision-makers. Empathy influences how a leader sets priorities.

Instead of focusing solely on what's urgent, empathetic leaders focus on what's important to the well-being of their people and the long-term mission. Empathy enhances team performance. When team members feel understood and appreciated, they are more likely to contribute fully, collaborate openly, and innovate freely. A culture of empathy begins with modeling. Leaders must show what it looks like to be present, to listen deeply, and to respond with humility.

Their example gives others permission to do the same. In education, empathy opens the door to restorative justice. Rather than defaulting to punishment, empathetic educators ask, 'What harm was done? What support does the student need to make it right?' In the workplace, empathy reduces burnout.

Leaders who check in regularly and create safe spaces for vulnerability help staff feel valued and seen, preventing emotional exhaustion. An empathetic organization is a resilient one. Because people know they are supported, they recover faster from setbacks, learn from failure, and approach new challenges with confidence. Empathy allows for greater inclusivity. Leaders who take the time to understand different lived experiences are better positioned to foster environments where everyone belongs and contributes.

When leaders ask their teams how they're doing—and truly listen—they build credibility. People follow leaders who care not just about outcomes, but about those responsible for achieving them. Empathy must be embedded in the DNA of leadership development. Emerging leaders should be taught not only how to lead projects, but how to lead people—with compassion, emotional intelligence, and cultural humility. Empathy invites reflection.

Leaders who cultivate it take time to reflect on how their actions affect others and how their intentions are perceived. This creates a feedback loop that promotes growth and awareness. Empathy builds team identity. When people feel understood and supported, they become more loyal to their organization and committed to its mission. Empathy fosters emotional investment.

For leaders with a background in education, empathy sharpens the ability to meet students where they are. It transforms instructional decisions from rigid routines into thoughtful responses to unique learning needs. Empathy in policy-making can shift entire systems. When leaders understand the struggles of underserved populations, they are more likely to craft policies that are just, equitable, and human-centered. Empathy reshapes leadership hierarchies.

In empathetic cultures, leadership becomes more relational and less positional. Influence is earned through authenticity and care rather than authority alone. At the heart of diversity, equity, and inclusion work is empathy. It helps leaders understand that equality is not sameness—it is about giving people what they need to succeed. Empathy changes how we define success.

Instead of valuing speed and output above all else, empathetic leadership values sustainability, growth, and well-being for everyone involved. In conflict resolution, empathy is a bridge. It de-escalates tension by acknowledging emotions and perspectives, and it paves the way for solutions rooted in understanding rather than domination. Empathy turns listening into leadership. By consistently tuning into what others are experiencing, leaders position themselves as trustworthy, grounded, and credible guides through uncertainty.

A culture of empathy cannot be manufactured; it must be cultivated. It requires intentional investment, ongoing modeling, and the courage to prioritize humanity in a world that often favors productivity. Empathy in action involves courageous vulnerability. Leaders who admit when they don't have all the answers or when they've made mistakes create environments of honesty and openness. Mentorship is a powerful expression of empathy.

When leaders invest in the growth of others by sharing experiences, offering guidance, and providing encouragement, they communicate deep care for future success. Empathy supports inclusive communication. It helps leaders choose language that welcomes instead of alienates, that empowers rather than diminishes, and that considers diverse audiences with respect. Culturally responsive leaders use empathy to uncover and celebrate the richness of different backgrounds, identities, and experiences. This awareness leads to better team collaboration and a more just workplace.

Empathy helps teams navigate transitions. Whether adapting to new leadership, restructuring roles, or managing external challenges, empathetic leadership ensures people feel secure and valued during change. Leadership development programs should include empathy training as a core component. Empathy is not just innate—it can be taught, practiced, and refined over time through reflection and real-life experiences. Empathy-driven leaders view accountability as a partnership.

They clarify expectations and support individuals in meeting them, understanding that success is a shared responsibility, not a one-sided demand. Empathy makes performance evaluations more humane. Rather than reducing people to numbers, empathetic leaders consider the full context of individual contributions and well-being when giving feedback. Empathy is vital in virtual and hybrid work environments. Without physical presence, leaders must become more intentional in how they connect, check in, and support team members across digital platforms.

Ultimately, empathy in action is a daily discipline. It is reflected in how we respond to conflict, how we celebrate others, how we lead meetings, and how we center people in all aspects of organizational life. Empathy in leadership is not just a philosophy; it's a framework for action. Leaders who center empathy in their approach develop stronger connections and produce more sustainable outcomes. One of the most underrated aspects of empathetic leadership is patience.

When leaders give people the time and space to process change or challenges, they honor individual pacing and reduce unnecessary pressure. In school administration, for instance, empathetic principals don't just evaluate teachers—they coach, mentor, and walk beside them. They ask what support looks like before offering judgment. Empathy elevates staff meetings from routine check-ins to meaningful dialogue. It encourages leaders to invite open feedback, address concerns directly, and offer encouragement tailored to team needs.

When leaders pair empathy with data, they gain deeper insights. They go beyond numbers to understand the stories behind performance metrics, which leads to better decision-making. Empathy in hiring and onboarding creates more inclusive environments. When new employees are met with understanding and grace, they feel empowered to contribute authentically from day one. In healthcare and social work, empathy is essential for preventing compassion fatigue.

Leaders who support frontline workers through active listening and mental health resources foster resilience and retention. Empathy enhances professional development. By tuning into team members' aspirations and barriers, leaders can tailor growth opportunities that are truly meaningful and motivating. Empathy creates a culture of belonging. It is the antidote to exclusion and the foundation for psychological safety, where people feel brave enough to speak up, challenge ideas, and show vulnerability.

At its highest level, empathy in action is leadership with soul. It is the difference between a workplace that extracts effort and one that inspires excellence through care, dignity, and mutual respect. Empathy is critical in shaping disciplinary practices in schools and organizations. Leaders who approach discipline through an empathetic lens focus on growth and understanding rather than punishment and shame. By understanding the root causes of behavior, empathetic leaders can craft interventions that address underlying issues rather than merely addressing symptoms.

This leads to long-term positive change and stronger relationships. Empathy also empowers team members to be empathetic themselves. When they see their leaders model active listening and respect, it becomes part of the organization's culture and peer-to-peer relationships improve. In community outreach and advocacy, empathy informs how messages are communicated. Campaigns grounded in empathy consider audience perspectives and seek to uplift rather than shame or alienate.

Empathetic leaders recognize that everyone carries unseen burdens. From family responsibilities to mental health struggles, an empathetic workplace allows individuals to be whole people, not just performers of tasks. One powerful act of empathy is simply checking in. Asking, 'How are you really doing?' and meaning it—without rushing to move on—can make someone feel deeply seen and supported. Empathy can serve as a compass in moments of ethical uncertainty.

When leaders take time to understand how decisions affect all stakeholders, they are more likely to choose a just and equitable path. Coaching through empathy involves more than just giving advice—it's about asking thoughtful questions, offering support without judgment, and walking alongside someone through their learning curve. Empathy is contagious. In a culture where empathy is embedded, individuals start looking out for each other more, offering help without being asked, and creating an unspoken network of care. Ultimately, empathy in action creates workplaces, schools, and communities that are not just successful—but humane, where people matter more than metrics, and dignity is never compromised for productivity.

Empathy can transform the way organizations respond to failure. Rather than assigning blame, empathetic leaders seek to understand context, foster learning, and use failure as a springboard for growth. Celebrating milestones with empathy means acknowledging both the achievement and the journey. Leaders who take time to recognize the emotional effort behind success deepen team loyalty and morale. Empathy makes space for difference.

It welcomes neurodiversity, emotional expression, and varied communication styles. In doing so, it expands the definition of what it means to be 'professional.' An empathetic mindset in leadership fosters generational understanding. Rather than assuming every generation should conform, empathetic leaders bridge gaps through listening, respect, and shared values. Empathy enhances the customer experience.

In businesses and nonprofits alike, understanding the needs, frustrations, and aspirations of those served results in more relevant solutions and greater trust. In boardrooms and leadership teams, empathy reshapes conversations. It encourages vulnerability, builds consensus, and prevents groupthink by validating diverse opinions. Training future leaders in empathy prepares them for the complexity of human systems. It ensures they enter leadership with not only strategy and vision, but also heart and relational skill.

Empathy helps mitigate the effects of bias. When leaders are attuned to the lived realities of marginalized groups, they're more likely to challenge inequities and foster a sense of belonging. Empathy deepens trust during organizational transitions, such as mergers or leadership changes. It helps leaders communicate transparently and guide their people through uncertainty with care. When empathy is part of an organization's mission, it becomes a guiding principle for hiring, program development, partnerships, and even financial decisions.

It becomes the heartbeat of the work. Empathy sharpens cultural intelligence. Leaders who immerse themselves in different cultural narratives become more adept at navigating global teams and multicultural partnerships. One of the most powerful aspects of empathy is its capacity to neutralize fear. When leaders lead with empathy, they replace apprehension with assurance and alienation with acceptance.

In times of societal unrest, empathy equips leaders to respond with both courage and compassion. It allows them to acknowledge pain, elevate voices, and take thoughtful action that aligns with core values. Empathy can be the foundation of ethical leadership. It urges decision-makers to look beyond bottom lines and assess the human cost and moral implications of their actions. In educational settings, teachers who employ empathetic strategies often see increased student engagement, lower behavioral issues, and improved academic outcomes.

Students thrive when they feel understood. Empathy is key in cross-functional collaboration. When departments operate with mutual respect and curiosity about one another's roles and pressures, organizational silos begin to break down. When leaders give empathetic feedback, it leads to growth rather than defensiveness. Constructive critique becomes a tool for development, not a trigger for fear or resentment.

Empathy encourages intergenerational mentorship. By valuing both wisdom and fresh perspectives, organizations create pathways for leadership continuity and innovation. Empathy strengthens resilience during crisis. It reminds teams they are not alone and that their efforts matter. This shared emotional support becomes a collective source of strength.

Finally, empathy makes leadership more human. In a world increasingly driven by automation and efficiency, empathy re-centers the importance of people—reminding us that leadership is, above all, a relationship. Empathy paves the way for transparency. Leaders who communicate honestly and with compassion earn the trust of their teams, even during difficult conversations or organizational shifts. A powerful outcome of empathy is psychological safety.

When people feel safe to express opinions and admit mistakes without fear of ridicule or punishment, innovation and collaboration flourish. Empathetic leaders understand the importance of celebrating individuality. They allow people to bring their full selves to work, embracing diverse strengths, identities, and communication styles. The best mentorships are rooted in empathy. Rather than imposing a one-size-fits-all model, empathetic mentors tailor their support to the mentee's personality, goals, and challenges.

Empathy shapes how we lead across lines of difference—whether cultural, generational, racial, or ideological. It invites humility, curiosity, and a willingness to learn from others' lived experiences. In educational reform, empathy enables leaders to craft policies that serve students, families, and educators more effectively by listening closely to those most impacted by change. Empathy isn't about agreeing with everyone—it's about seeking to understand. This mindset transforms dialogue, lowers defensiveness, and fosters respect even amid disagreement.

Empathy enhances service delivery. Whether in healthcare, government, or customer service, providers who lead with empathy respond more holistically and build trust with those they serve. In community leadership, empathy bridges social gaps. It motivates outreach that's respectful, relevant, and responsive to the unique realities of each neighborhood or group. Ultimately, empathy in action is not a soft skill—it's a strategic advantage.

It humanizes institutions, strengthens morale, and anchors leadership in purpose and humanity. Empathy influences how leaders shape workplace norms. By emphasizing emotional awareness and mutual respect, they create environments where people feel valued and motivated to contribute fully. Empathetic leaders pay attention to burnout signals and act preemptively. They check in with their teams, redistribute workload when needed, and advocate for systemic changes that support wellness.

Empathy plays a key role in succession planning. Leaders who care deeply about people's potential identify and nurture future leaders based on readiness and values alignment—not just technical skills. When a crisis strikes, empathetic leadership is often the difference between panic and poise. People look to leaders not only for direction but also for emotional grounding, compassion, and stability. Empathy helps leaders embrace vulnerability.

It takes strength to ask for feedback, admit when things aren't working, or pivot a strategy based on team input. These moments deepen trust and credibility. In conflict mediation, empathy fosters deeper resolution. When opposing parties feel heard and validated, they are more willing to move toward compromise and long-term reconciliation. Empathy empowers inclusive innovation.

When all voices are welcomed and considered, teams generate more creative, well-rounded solutions that reflect real needs and broader perspectives. Leaders practicing empathy listen not only to words, but also to tone, silence, and body language. This deeper attunement allows them to respond more fully to what others may struggle to articulate. Empathy encourages consistency. When leaders treat everyone with fairness and grace—regardless of rank or role—it sets a tone of reliability that reinforces psychological safety and team cohesion.

Above all, empathy reinforces a people-first mindset. In every decision—from hiring to communication to strategy—empathetic leaders ask, 'How will this affect the people who matter most?' Empathy fosters ethical responsibility. Leaders who see the impact of their decisions through the lens of others are more likely to lead with integrity and fairness. In educational leadership, empathetic administrators understand the diverse challenges students and teachers face.

They use this insight to create policies that support equity and engagement. Empathy deepens community partnerships. When leaders engage local voices and seek to understand the needs of neighborhoods, they build relationships rooted in trust and shared purpose. Organizations that prioritize empathy in leadership often see lower turnover and higher satisfaction. Employees are more likely to stay where they feel genuinely heard and supported.

Empathy also fuels adaptability. Leaders who remain attuned to team morale and emotional feedback are better equipped to adjust strategies in ways that are responsive and humane. Listening with empathy allows for deeper understanding than simply waiting to respond. This shift from reaction to reflection strengthens interpersonal dynamics and decision-making. Empathy is key in addressing systemic barriers.

Leaders who approach issues through the lens of compassion recognize and dismantle structures that exclude or disadvantage marginalized groups. Workplaces that model empathy often extend it outward, shaping customer and client interactions in more thoughtful, inclusive, and impactful ways. Leaders grounded in empathy view their teams as people first, not just producers. This mindset informs everything from meeting formats to performance evaluations to team celebrations. At its best, empathy in action becomes a ripple effect—beginning with leadership, flowing through the team, and extending into every aspect of the organization's mission and culture.

Empathy promotes inclusive decision-making by urging leaders to seek input from those who may otherwise be overlooked. This collaboration creates more balanced, relevant outcomes. When leaders ask for feedback and truly listen, they model humility and respect—two essential traits that build strong, cohesive teams. Empathy drives the courage to ask, 'What can I do better?' Empathy builds bridges across departments and hierarchies.

It reminds organizations that success isn't about silos but about synergy, where each role is seen and valued. In education, teachers who lead with empathy manage classrooms with compassion. They discipline to teach—not to punish—and provide second chances that affirm student worth. Empathetic leadership addresses the emotional toll of change. Whether it's a curriculum shift or a major reorganization, leaders who validate feelings and guide with steadiness ease transitions.

In high-stress environments, empathy de-escalates tension. When tempers rise, a calm and compassionate response diffuses conflict and preserves dignity. Empathy doesn't mean lowering standards—it means raising awareness. Leaders can hold high expectations while being attuned to individual circumstances and needs. Empathy and justice go hand in hand.

Understanding someone's story doesn't excuse poor behavior, but it does offer context that informs fair and constructive responses. Empathy in action is leadership with listening at its core. It is about showing up fully, setting aside assumptions, and embracing others not in spite of their struggles, but because of them. As a legacy trait, empathy ensures the impact of leadership lives beyond titles and tenures. It leaves behind not just results, but relationships—rooted in care, courage, and connection.

Empathy is the cornerstone of restorative practices. In both schools and workplaces, it allows individuals to take accountability in ways that heal rather than harm. When leaders create space for vulnerability, they encourage others to share openly, knowing they will be received with care rather than judgment. Empathetic leadership resists the urge to rush to solutions. It understands that sometimes, the most powerful act is simply to be present, offering a listening ear without immediate answers.

Empathy empowers team members to speak up about inequities. A leader who fosters safety through compassion invites truth—even when it's hard to hear. In global contexts, empathy cultivates diplomacy. When people from different nations and perspectives approach dialogue with respect and curiosity, understanding takes root. Empathy strengthens virtual collaboration.

In an era of remote work, it fuels intentional communication and acknowledges the personal circumstances that shape digital engagement. Empathy amplifies advocacy. When leaders center lived experience in their messaging, they create movements that resonate more deeply and inspire collective action. Mentorship grounded in empathy often creates lifelong influence. Empathetic mentors see beyond performance—they nurture potential, character, and confidence.

Even in high-stakes environments like emergency response or military operations, empathy has a role. It reminds leaders to safeguard human dignity, even when urgency dominates decision-making. Ultimately, empathy allows us to lead not from ego, but from service. It reminds us that our influence is not measured by power, but by how people feel in our presence—and how they grow as a result of it. Empathy builds unity across sectors.

Whether in healthcare, education, business, or public service, the shared value of understanding and compassion fosters collaboration that transcends silos. When leaders model empathy during team conflict, they shift the focus from blame to shared responsibility, allowing solutions to emerge from a place of mutual respect. Empathy ensures that performance evaluations are more than metrics—they become conversations about development, goals, and personal well-being. Empathetic teams engage in reflective practices that deepen learning. They debrief not only on what went well or poorly, but also on how people felt and what they needed during each stage of a project.

Empathy reshapes how we define success. Instead of solely focusing on output, leaders ask how sustainable and empowering the work feels to those involved. In servant leadership, empathy is not a tactic but a way of being. It defines how power is shared, how trust is cultivated, and how people are treated at every level. Empathy nurtures interfaith and intercultural understanding.

In diverse communities, this quality enables leaders to foster cohesion without erasing difference. A culture of empathy resists burnout.

It normalizes breaks, encourages mental health support, and values people beyond their productivity. Empathy encourages curiosity. When we care to understand others deeply, we become more open-minded, better listeners, and more thoughtful communicators.

Finally, empathy ensures that our leadership reflects the humanity we wish to inspire. It transforms goals into legacies, policies into values, and vision into collective empowerment. Empathy teaches leaders how to be emotionally agile. They learn to hold space for others' emotions without being consumed by them, balancing compassion with clarity. In times of transition, empathy honors the grief that may accompany change.

It allows people to let go of what was while preparing their hearts and minds for what will be. Empathy is key to trauma-informed leadership. It equips leaders to recognize and respond to signs of distress with care, avoiding retraumatization and fostering healing. Empathy makes inclusion authentic. It helps leaders see beyond tokenism and performative acts, ensuring diverse voices are not only heard but integrated into decision-making.

Leaders who practice empathy often build informal support systems within teams. These networks strengthen morale, create belonging, and sustain people during high-stress periods. Empathy drives proactive communication. It encourages leaders to share information transparently, anticipating how news—good or bad—will emotionally impact their teams. When teams hit roadblocks, empathy redirects focus from failure to learning.

It replaces shame with curiosity and encourages growth without fear. Empathy fosters allyship. Leaders stand beside those facing adversity, using their influence to advocate for justice, resources, and recognition. In personal development, empathy sharpens self-awareness. It helps leaders reflect on how their actions and words affect others, and adjust their approach for greater alignment.

Ultimately, empathy in action becomes the heart of transformative leadership. It enables not just influence, but impact that is meaningful, lasting, and deeply human. Empathy guides how we respond to feedback. Instead of becoming defensive, empathetic leaders listen with the intent to understand and grow, modeling teachability and emotional intelligence. In mentorship, empathy fuels the courage to ask powerful questions.

It's not about giving all the answers but about helping others discover their own clarity through compassion. Empathy improves how we design systems. When we ask, 'Who is this not working for?' and lead with the stories behind the statistics, policies become more human-centered and equitable. Empathetic leadership honors the whole person—not just the employee, student, or team member. It respects the invisible weight people carry outside their roles and creates space for grace.

In moments of conflict, empathy gives leaders the wisdom to pause. That pause can prevent misunderstanding, de-escalate emotion, and allow thoughtful, compassionate resolution. Empathy in education revolutionizes school climate. It leads to fewer suspensions, stronger teacher-student relationships, and learning environments where students feel safe to take risks. Empathetic leadership doesn't just create followers—it creates other leaders.

By modeling compassion, respect, and active listening, it inspires others to lead with humanity too. Empathy equips leaders to handle moral dilemmas. When the right choice isn't easy or popular, they lean into people-first principles and make decisions that reflect shared values. True empathy asks us to slow down. In a fast-paced world, it reminds us that people aren't problems to solve but humans to connect with—and that connection is where real transformation begins.

As a leadership legacy, empathy speaks volumes not through titles or accolades, but through the memories people hold of being seen, heard, and deeply valued. Empathy transforms evaluations into opportunities for growth. Instead of focusing solely on outcomes, leaders consider the human context that shaped the results and offer support accordingly. Empathetic communication shifts the emphasis from correction to connection. Leaders give feedback with the intention of uplift, making it more likely to be heard and acted upon.

When empathy drives vision, organizations become more than businesses—they become movements that make people feel they belong to something greater than themselves. Empathy leads to policies that protect—not punish. It encourages leaders to design systems that anticipate needs, remove barriers, and create environments where people can thrive. A culture built on empathy becomes a magnet for talent. People want to work where their voices are honored, where compassion is the norm, and where well-being is a strategic priority.

Empathy is a multiplier of trust. With every kind gesture, every listening ear, and every moment of patience, it compounds, weaving a culture that is resilient, open, and unshakable. In global leadership, empathy bridges continents. It honors local wisdom, adapts to cultural nuance, and promotes unity across borders through mutual understanding. Empathy ignites transformational teaching.

Educators who understand their students' emotional needs foster engagement, retention, and a lifelong love of learning. When embedded in leadership training, empathy shapes future change agents who know that results matter—but people matter more. The ultimate gift of empathy is legacy. Long after initiatives end or roles change, people remember how a leader made them feel—seen, valued, and empowered to rise. Empathy paves the way for sustainable innovation.

When people feel emotionally secure, they are more likely to take creative risks that lead to breakthrough ideas. Leaders who lead with empathy understand that progress doesn't always follow a straight line. They honor the emotional journey that accompanies growth, especially during challenging times. Ultimately, empathy is not a soft skill—it is a strategic imperative. It builds cultures where people thrive, organizations succeed, and communities flourish. As leaders, we must strive to be the kind of people whose presence brings comfort and whose leadership ignites the best in others. Empathy is the vehicle that makes this possible.

Chapter 9: The Momentum of Integrity

Integrity is the engine that powers long-term influence. While charisma may capture attention and talent may open doors, it is integrity that keeps doors open and builds sustainable trust.

In leadership, integrity means aligning words with actions. It's the daily commitment to do what's right—even when it's inconvenient, unpopular, or unseen. People are drawn to consistency. When leaders uphold their values regardless of audience or outcome, they create a sense of reliability that fuels loyalty and respect. Integrity builds momentum because it compounds over time.

Each honest action, each ethical decision, becomes a building block in a reputation that others can depend on. When leaders model integrity, they give their teams permission to do the same. It creates a culture where accountability is not feared but welcomed as a marker of excellence. In moments of pressure, integrity becomes the true test of character. It's easy to act ethically when the stakes are low—but real leadership is revealed when tough choices must be made.

Integrity demands self-awareness. Leaders must regularly examine their motives and choices, ensuring that ambition never overtakes principle. Organizations that prioritize integrity see benefits in performance and morale. When people trust their leaders, they are more willing to take initiative, collaborate, and stay engaged. In education, integrity shows up when educators advocate for what's best for students, even when it challenges the status quo or demands personal sacrifice.

Ultimately, integrity is not a single act—it's a lifestyle. It is the momentum that turns leadership from a position into a purpose, and success from a moment into a legacy. Integrity anchors a leader's credibility. Without it, even the most compelling strategies or visions fall flat, as people struggle to trust intentions or follow directions. It is through integrity that leaders earn the benefit of the doubt.

When mistakes happen—and they inevitably do—followers are more forgiving when there's a strong history of honesty and fairness. The momentum of integrity strengthens teams by encouraging truth-telling. When employees see that integrity is valued, they're more likely to speak up, admit errors, and propose bold ideas. Integrity is a bridge between power and purpose. It transforms leadership from self-interest into service, shifting the focus from personal gain to collective good.

In times of crisis, integrity becomes the compass that prevents panic. Leaders who remain anchored in truth provide reassurance and direction, calming chaos through steadiness. True integrity is tested not when it's easy to be ethical, but when cutting corners might offer a quicker reward. Leaders of principle resist shortcuts and demonstrate that doing what's right is always worth it. Organizations that invest in ethical leadership training reap long-term rewards—reduced risk, improved retention, and stronger community partnerships.

In school systems, integrity is modeled in how educators treat their students, how administrators allocate resources, and how districts remain transparent with families. Integrity is not just for the workplace; it is essential in our personal lives as well. The consistency we show in all spheres of life builds a reputation that precedes us wherever we go. Ultimately, the momentum of integrity is the invisible force that accelerates trust, deepens impact, and sustains influence through the ever-changing landscapes of leadership. Leaders who embody integrity influence more than just their teams—they influence the entire culture.

Integrity is contagious; it sets a tone that becomes the standard. A culture of integrity results in more open communication. When people feel safe being honest, they bring forward innovative ideas, share critical feedback, and prevent small issues from becoming major problems. Integrity builds character from the inside out. It shapes decision-making and habits, even in the absence of external oversight or immediate consequences.

In community leadership, integrity reinforces equity. It ensures that leaders serve all constituents with fairness and that policies do not benefit the privileged few at the expense of the many. In the corporate world, leaders who act with integrity earn brand loyalty. Customers trust companies whose executives consistently demonstrate transparency, fairness, and social responsibility. The momentum of integrity also shields against burnout.

Leaders who stay aligned with their core values are less likely to compromise themselves for external validation, allowing them to lead with peace of mind. One of the most powerful outcomes of integrity is clarity. Leaders are better able to navigate complexity and ambiguity when their moral compass is well-calibrated and unshakable. Integrity builds a foundation for inclusive leadership. It compels leaders to ensure that every voice is heard, every perspective is valued, and every action is rooted in justice.

When teaching integrity to young people, modeling is more effective than lectures. Students learn by watching how adults handle adversity, resolve conflict, and follow through on commitments. The momentum of integrity inspires legacy thinking. It encourages leaders to act in ways that their future selves—and future generations—can be proud of. Leaders with integrity are trusted to make decisions even when others don't fully understand the process.

That trust stems from a track record of consistency, fairness, and honesty. Integrity fosters emotional intelligence. Leaders who act ethically are often more attuned to how their choices impact others emotionally and relationally. The most effective change agents are those grounded in integrity. They don't chase trends or popularity—they remain committed to long-term transformation, even when the process is slow.

In academic institutions, integrity manifests in academic honesty, fair grading practices, and equitable discipline. When educators and administrators lead with integrity, they reinforce the importance of ethical conduct in all areas of life. Integrity is often measured when no one is watching. What leaders do in private—how they treat support staff, handle sensitive information, or manage personal responsibilities—reveals their true character. The momentum of integrity allows for meaningful reflection.

Leaders who consistently reflect on their behavior and decisions grow in self-awareness and improve their leadership practice. Crisis reveals character, and integrity is the backbone of character. During disruptions, people gravitate toward those who lead with calm, honesty, and unwavering ethics. In a digitally connected world, integrity must also show up online. Leaders must ensure that their digital presence—social media, email, messaging—matches their values and upholds their professional reputation.

In mentoring relationships, integrity allows for vulnerability. When mentors are honest about their own failures and lessons, they create safe spaces for others to grow without fear of judgment. The long game of leadership is not about immediate rewards but enduring impact. Integrity ensures that the influence a leader leaves behind continues to inspire and uplift others long after they've moved on. Integrity also nurtures resilience.

Leaders grounded in principle bounce back more effectively from setbacks because they're guided by purpose, not just outcomes. Empowered teams are often led by people of integrity. When leaders are truthful, they enable their teams to function with autonomy and confidence, without micromanagement or fear. Young leaders especially benefit from early modeling of integrity. Exposure to ethical decision-making in their formative years creates a moral framework that will influence generations.

Integrity elevates everyday interactions. It shows up in how meetings are run, how credit is given, how disagreements are managed, and how people are recognized for their work. There is a direct link between integrity and transparency. Leaders who embrace integrity communicate clearly, avoid manipulation, and foster organizational openness. Integrity strengthens partnerships.

Whether in schools, nonprofits, or businesses, collaborations thrive when all parties feel that promises will be honored and values will be respected. In the nonprofit sector, integrity determines credibility. Funders and community members place trust—and resources—into leaders who prove their honesty and accountability. The momentum of integrity builds internal alignment. Leaders who stay true to their values experience less cognitive dissonance, which improves mental health and decision-making clarity.

Ethical lapses, no matter how minor, can unravel trust. That's why integrity must be seen as a discipline—one that is practiced daily and embedded into the culture at all levels. In truth, the greatest leaders are not remembered for their accomplishments alone, but for the integrity with which they carried them out. That's the essence of lasting influence. A leader's integrity influences every tier of the organization, from the executive suite to frontline employees.

It sets the expectations not only for behavior but for decision-making, transparency, and accountability. In the educational environment, integrity impacts grading policies, attendance protocols, and even the way educators handle disciplinary measures. Every decision becomes a chance to reinforce fairness and consistency. Integrity is not reactive; it is proactive. It anticipates the consequences of decisions and considers how to align with moral standards before challenges arise.

As integrity builds momentum, it influences institutional reputation. Schools, companies, and nonprofits led by individuals of character become known for ethical excellence, attracting partners and supporters who share those values. Leaders who emphasize integrity foster strong moral reasoning in their teams. When individuals are invited into ethical conversations, they develop the capacity to think beyond compliance toward genuine responsibility. The momentum of integrity leads to courage.

Ethical leaders are not afraid to challenge unjust norms or disrupt flawed traditions. They act with the conviction that long-term justice outweighs short-term popularity. In professional development, integrity-based leadership models are key. They shift the focus from mere skill acquisition to value-centered growth that equips people for conscientious leadership. Leaders who navigate with integrity understand that trust is not a given—it is earned, preserved, and repaired through consistent ethical conduct.

One of the hidden powers of integrity is its ability to inspire others to elevate their own character. Witnessing someone else's moral clarity often prompts reflection and transformation. At its core, the momentum of integrity isn't about perfection—it's about direction. Leaders committed to continuous ethical growth build environments where honesty, respect, and accountability thrive. Integrity brings alignment between what is said and what is done.

When this alignment is visible, it strengthens confidence within the organization and removes barriers to collaboration. In community leadership, integrity builds coalitions that last. Coalitions forged through trust and shared principles are more resilient to political shifts and public scrutiny. Ethical leadership doesn't require perfection. It requires the humility to admit when you're wrong and the strength to make it right.

The power of integrity is amplified when practiced during the most difficult moments. When reputations are on the line, when hard truths must be spoken—these are the crucibles where integrity shines brightest. Educational leaders face constant scrutiny, and integrity is their safeguard. Whether navigating policy decisions or parental concerns, integrity provides clarity and courage. In leadership transitions, the legacy of integrity is often the most enduring.

It leaves a blueprint for successors to follow and a moral compass for the institution to retain. Leaders who model integrity cultivate resilience within their teams. People who know their leaders will support them in doing the right thing are more willing to innovate and take risks. Integrity is foundational to conflict resolution. By addressing disagreements with honesty, fairness, and a willingness to listen, leaders foster environments where conflict strengthens rather than fractures relationships.

Transparency, a close ally of integrity, allows teams to understand not just decisions but the reasoning behind them. This builds ownership, not just compliance. At every level, from family to global governance, integrity builds the bridges that connect people, ideas, and actions toward common good. Integrity enhances credibility, and credibility multiplies influence. A leader known for integrity can mobilize others faster and more effectively because their motives are rarely questioned.

The workplace becomes more efficient when integrity is a cultural norm. Time spent managing drama, checking facts, or second-guessing decisions is significantly reduced. Students in classrooms led by educators with integrity experience not only academic instruction but moral formation. They learn how to be good citizens by observing how teachers handle praise, discipline, and pressure. Integrity also plays a role in how leaders handle success.

Ethical leaders share credit generously, acknowledge the contributions of others, and remain grounded in purpose rather than ego. In the digital age, integrity must be extended to data handling, online communication, and social engagement. A single lapse in these areas can compromise trust that took years to build. Leaders who build momentum through integrity also attract top talent. People want to work in places where ethics aren't negotiable and where doing the right thing is part of the everyday expectation.

A key marker of integrity is how leaders respond to feedback. Do they listen? Do they grow? Leaders who remain teachable increase their influence and expand the organization's capacity for excellence.

Integrity should not be a badge worn in public and discarded in private.

True integrity is integrated—woven through all aspects of a leader's identity and behavior. Training in ethics should be continuous. Organizations benefit from regular reflection, workshops, and scenarios that strengthen moral decision-making and reinforce a shared ethical vision. Ultimately, the momentum of integrity enables leaders to sleep well at night, knowing they've acted with honesty, honored their word, and left a legacy that will outlast their title. Integrity creates the emotional safety needed for innovation.

When people know they won't be shamed or deceived, they're more likely to experiment and express unconventional ideas. Leaders who consistently practice integrity often cultivate more diverse and inclusive teams. People from different backgrounds feel respected and valued in environments where fairness and transparency prevail. It's important to distinguish between image management and integrity. While the former prioritizes perception, the latter is rooted in principle.

Leaders driven by integrity make choices that matter, even when no one is watching. Ethical leadership is not about being liked—it's about being trustworthy. Integrity may not always make a leader popular in the short term, but it guarantees long-term respect. Integrity impacts financial stewardship. Leaders who are accountable with money, time, and resources demonstrate that they can be trusted with responsibility at every level.

Building a culture of integrity starts with small decisions. These daily moments—how a leader greets a colleague, how they respond to inconvenience, how they handle confidential information—build a mosaic of trust. Integrity prevents the normalization of dysfunction. In toxic environments, a single leader of character can interrupt cycles of deceit and create a pathway toward renewal. Leaders who commit to integrity don't just influence their peers; they become mentors by example.

Their choices model the kind of character development that shapes future generations. One of the lesser-discussed benefits of integrity is clarity of purpose. Leaders who lead with integrity often have a deeper sense of calling, which sustains them through obstacles and uncertainty. At its best, the momentum of integrity can transform not just organizations but entire communities. When ethical leadership becomes the norm, it raises the bar for everyone involved.

In boardrooms and classrooms alike, integrity cultivates influence that does not rely on force or manipulation. It builds authority grounded in respect, not fear. When leaders choose integrity, they create a ripple effect. Others around them are encouraged to raise their own ethical standards, leading to a widespread shift in culture. The power of apology is rooted in integrity.

Leaders who admit fault and take steps to repair damage not only maintain trust—they deepen it. Integrity aligns leadership with humanity. It allows leaders to remain empathetic while staying grounded in principle, avoiding the pitfall of becoming detached or authoritarian. In high-stakes environments, integrity can feel like a liability. But over time, it becomes an asset that distinguishes great leaders from those who simply chase results.

Leaders with integrity create predictability in unpredictable times. Their consistency becomes an anchor when everything else is in flux. Ethical decision-making is not just about choosing right over wrong—it's about choosing better over good, especially when faced with multiple acceptable options. One challenge of integrity is navigating gray areas. The most trusted leaders are those who engage in open dialogue, gather diverse perspectives, and make informed decisions rooted in values.

Integrity makes delegation more effective. Team members are more likely to embrace responsibility and perform with excellence when they believe their work is valued and judged fairly. The legacy of integrity is not confined to professional spaces. It extends into families, friendships, and communities, where trust, truth, and consistency are cornerstones of meaningful connection. At the intersection of leadership and legacy lies integrity.

It is the invisible thread that binds a leader's intentions to their outcomes. Leaders who lead with integrity are more likely to create sustainable systems. Shortcuts and deception may yield quick wins, but only integrity ensures long-term viability. In conflict mediation, a leader's integrity can neutralize tension. People are more likely to compromise and find common ground when they believe the process is fair and the facilitator is trustworthy.

Ethical leadership helps organizations withstand scrutiny. Whether from stakeholders, the public, or internal reviews, leaders of integrity have nothing to hide and everything to model. The relationship between transparency and morale is often underappreciated. Teams thrive when they understand why decisions are made and trust that they're in good hands. Schools, businesses, and nonprofits led by people of integrity become magnets for partnerships.

Others want to collaborate with leaders whose word can be counted on and whose vision is principled. The consistency of integrity forms the blueprint for excellence. It becomes the standard by which quality, communication, and relationships are measured. Integrity encourages leaders to hold themselves to higher standards, even when external expectations are low. This internal compass distinguishes trailblazers from placeholders.

In moments of pressure, integrity is not a burden—it's a relief. It removes the stress of second-guessing and the anxiety of being caught in compromise. Ultimately, the momentum of integrity doesn't just carry leaders forward. It carries others with them, building communities, teams, and cultures that thrive on trust. Leaders of integrity are also stewards of time.

They honor schedules, meet deadlines, and respect others' commitments, reinforcing a culture of reliability. Integrity fosters psychological safety in teams. People feel secure to speak up, contribute ideas, and raise concerns when they trust that honesty will be met with respect. One of the most subtle forms of leadership is modeling integrity under stress. In moments of chaos or crisis, maintaining ethical grounding inspires calm and discipline in others.

In student leadership programs, teaching integrity as a daily practice equips young people to navigate peer pressure and become principled influencers. Organizations that prioritize integrity in hiring and promotions avoid the corrosive effects of favoritism, politics, and inconsistency. Integrity becomes tangible when leaders live it out in routine decisions—like how they spend budget surpluses, whom they include in planning, or how they respond to failure. The cost of compromising integrity is rarely just personal—it reverberates throughout teams and institutions, weakening cohesion and trust. Integrity allows leaders to say no with confidence.

Boundaries grounded in values provide clarity that prevents overextension and burnout. In strategic planning, integrity ensures that goals align not only with profit or achievement, but with purpose and impact. The momentum of integrity is cumulative. Each ethical choice builds on the last, creating a legacy that speaks louder than any title or accomplishment. The ripple effect of integrity stretches far beyond the leader.

It influences the way team members interact with clients, peers, and even competitors. Integrity in leadership promotes alignment between mission and method. A leader who operates ethically ensures that how goals are achieved matters just as much as achieving them. In mentoring relationships, integrity builds trust quickly. When mentees see consistency in word and deed, they are more likely to model those values in their own careers.

When policies reflect integrity, they protect not just the organization but the people it serves. Clear ethical guidelines prevent exploitation and enhance fairness. The language of integrity includes transparency, accountability, and humility. Leaders fluent in these values communicate with clarity and conviction. Integrity-based leadership produces long-term returns.

While the initial path may be slower or more challenging, the resulting loyalty, trust, and stability are invaluable. In educational settings, integrity becomes a model for youth who are still shaping their identities. Students don't just learn facts—they absorb behaviors. The ability to apologize and take corrective action when needed is a crucial expression of integrity. It separates principled leaders from prideful ones.

A culture of integrity invites honest feedback. When people feel safe to speak candidly, leaders are better informed and organizations make wiser decisions. At its highest expression, the momentum of integrity helps people become not just better professionals but better humans—committed to justice, truth, and the greater good. When integrity is woven into every decision, leaders don't just manage—they inspire. Their consistency becomes a beacon for others navigating uncertainty.

Integrity guards against corruption, not just in finances but in relationships, communication, and intent. It's a moral firewall that protects both individuals and institutions. Leaders committed to integrity value truth more than convenience. They embrace difficult conversations and don't shy away from the discomfort that growth requires. The most enduring legacies are often built not on grand achievements, but on everyday choices grounded in honesty and fairness.

In high-functioning teams, integrity is assumed, not questioned. It becomes part of the air people breathe, shaping expectations and empowering autonomy. Integrity enables leaders to navigate power without abuse. It keeps influence grounded in service rather than self-interest. Communities thrive when civic leaders uphold integrity.

From local governments to grassroots organizations, ethical leadership promotes unity and shared purpose. Even in fiercely competitive industries, companies led by integrity-centered executives set a standard that others seek to follow. Integrity isn't inherited—it's cultivated. Leaders must invest in their own moral growth just as intentionally as they do their professional development. The true momentum of integrity is generational.

It doesn't just impact today's decisions—it shapes the values and expectations of those who follow in your footsteps. Leaders who embody integrity often earn loyalty that no incentive or policy can buy. People stay committed to missions when they trust the person at the helm. The test of true integrity often comes in moments when no one else is watching. How a leader handles private decisions defines their public reputation in time.

Integrity inspires the courage to speak truth to power. It empowers leaders at every level to stand up for what is right, even when it's unpopular or risky. In academic leadership, integrity ensures that student success metrics are not manipulated and that every achievement reflects real growth. Without integrity, success is hollow. With it, even small wins are deeply meaningful, because they were achieved without compromising core values.

Leaders who lead with integrity are resilient in the face of failure. They own their mistakes, learn from them, and turn them into platforms for growth. A culture of integrity eliminates the need for micromanagement. When team members trust that values are shared, oversight becomes guidance rather than control. In faith-based and nonprofit leadership, integrity is foundational.

It assures stakeholders that their contributions support work aligned with the organization's stated mission. Integrity also fuels innovation. When people aren't afraid of retribution for failed ideas, they take creative risks that can lead to breakthroughs. When the going gets tough, integrity becomes a compass. It helps leaders make decisions not based on fear or pressure, but on what aligns with who they are and what they stand for.

When integrity becomes an organizational value, it influences hiring, partnerships, and customer relations. Every relationship is shaped by the expectation of honesty and mutual respect. Leaders with integrity don't just manage crises—they prepare for them. Their plans reflect foresight and fairness, not just compliance or convenience. Integrity invites accountability.

Leaders welcome feedback, audits, and evaluation because they prioritize truth over image. The most admired leaders are often not those who never fall, but those who rise after failure with humility and transparency. Consistency in leadership builds morale. When people know what to expect from their leaders, anxiety decreases and focus improves. Integrity means aligning personal behavior with organizational vision.

Leaders become the living example of what they want their team to embody. In communities facing systemic challenges, leaders of integrity bring hope. Their honesty and advocacy remind others that progress is possible without sacrificing principles. Integrity leads to clarity. Ethical leaders communicate directly, make decisions efficiently, and avoid the paralysis of second-guessing driven by ulterior motives.

When values are tested, leaders of integrity remain grounded. Their identity is rooted not in popularity or prestige but in purpose. Ultimately, the momentum of integrity is about legacy. It outlives the leader and continues to shape the culture and conscience of those they've influenced. Integrity is often what separates leaders who are remembered from those who are forgotten.

A title may fade, but character leaves a lasting impression. Team members led by people of integrity are more likely to adopt ethical standards in their own work, creating a multiplier effect that strengthens the organization from within. A commitment to truth can be costly in the short term, but in the long run, it yields dividends in credibility, reputation, and peace of mind. Integrity fosters ownership. Employees who trust their leaders are more inclined to take initiative, admit mistakes, and strive for continuous improvement.

Leaders who rely on manipulation, half-truths, or spin eventually lose their effectiveness. People grow tired of deciphering intent and begin to disengage. The most trustworthy leaders are those whose personal and professional lives align. They do not compartmentalize their values—they live them holistically. Integrity is not just about what you say—it's about what you tolerate.

Allowing unethical behavior to persist undermines a leader's own credibility. In times of uncertainty, integrity becomes a source of calm. Knowing your decisions reflect your values eliminates the stress of performing for approval. Leadership built on integrity attracts and retains high-caliber talent. Professionals want to be part of teams where honesty, fairness, and mutual respect are non-negotiable.

As leaders reflect on their journeys, many find that the moments they're proudest of are not the most lucrative or public—but the most ethical. Integrity gives rise to influence that endures beyond a leader's presence. Those who follow remember not just what a leader did, but how they made decisions. The culture of an organization is shaped as much by what is permitted as by what is promoted. Integrity demands vigilance in both.

Every time a leader chooses honesty over convenience, they reinforce a standard. These moments may seem small, but they are the bricks of a strong ethical foundation. Integrity makes leaders approachable. People are more willing to bring forward concerns, new ideas, or challenges when they trust they won't be met with defensiveness or deceit. Ethical decision-making is not just a moral issue—it's a strategic advantage.

It attracts partners, funders, and collaborators who value values. In schools and educational institutions, integrity transforms classrooms into communities of trust. Students thrive when they know fairness guides every decision. The momentum of integrity compounds over time. Each principled choice builds the confidence to make the next one, even in more complex situations.

Leaders must resist the temptation to sacrifice long-term respect for short-term gain. Integrity is the asset that appreciates with every ethical choice. When employees see their leaders acting with integrity, they are more likely to report wrongdoing and uphold policies—creating a safer, stronger workplace. To lead with integrity is to accept that you may walk alone sometimes. But the impact of that walk echoes through generations who benefit from your example.

Integrity empowers a leader to lead without manipulation. Influence is earned through trust, not coercion or secrecy. When a team knows their leader stands on principles, they are more likely to step forward in difficult times, motivated by shared purpose rather than obligation. Integrity is the thread that connects leadership to legacy. It ensures that what a leader builds today remains strong tomorrow.

In the world of entrepreneurship, integrity builds brand loyalty. Consumers are increasingly drawn to companies whose values align with their own. Integrity requires self-awareness. Leaders must regularly reflect on whether their actions still align with their stated mission and vision. Leaders who demonstrate integrity are not afraid to challenge the status quo when it conflicts with ethical standards.

Integrity breeds resilience. When plans fall apart or criticism arises, leaders with integrity stand firm because their foundation is unshakable. The courage to walk away from unethical opportunities is a defining mark of leadership integrity. Not every open door should be entered. Integrity is contagious.

As one leader models it, others are inspired to raise their own standards, creating a ripple effect throughout an organization. To lead with integrity is to believe that who you are is just as important as what you do—and that belief is what sustains meaningful leadership. Integrity is the groundwork for sustainable innovation. When people feel morally secure, they think more creatively and collaborate more openly. Every ethical decision adds to a reservoir of trust that leaders draw from during moments of challenge.

Without it, even good ideas face skepticism. When leaders choose integrity over expedience, they build reputations that withstand scrutiny, change, and the passage of time. Integrity brings alignment between public image and private identity. This congruence fuels a leader's confidence and authentic presence. In complex systems, integrity helps simplify decision-making.

If a choice violates core values, it's immediately disqualified—no further analysis required. Integrity isn't about perfection; it's about consistency. Leaders who fall short but return to their values show the strength of character that people respect. Organizations that prioritize integrity foster cultures where inclusion, fairness, and transparency naturally thrive. A leader's silence in the face of wrongdoing can be louder than words.

Integrity requires the courage to speak when it would be easier to look away. When practiced daily, integrity becomes intuitive. Leaders begin to anticipate the ethical dimensions of decisions before they act. Ultimately, integrity allows leaders to rest easy. The weight of leadership becomes lighter when carried with a clean conscience and a clear purpose.

In every field—education, business, nonprofit, government—the leaders most remembered are those who never abandoned their moral compass. Integrity fosters followership rooted in admiration, not fear. People willingly follow those who lead with honor. When policy and practice align with ethical standards, organizations gain credibility that cannot be faked or fast-tracked. Integrity draws boundaries that preserve energy and prevent burnout.

When you're not pretending, you're not drained by maintaining a false front. The greatest measure of a leader's success is not in titles earned, but in the values upheld during the journey. Integrity does not need to shout. It speaks in the calm certainty of decisions made for the right reasons, even when no one is watching. As a society, our most trusted institutions are built upon the quiet, steady work of individuals who held fast to principles through chaos and change.

A life led with integrity becomes a legacy. Its impact multiplies as others are inspired to do the same, creating a continuum of positive influence. Let integrity not just be what you do when it's hard, but who you are when it's easy. Make it your leadership rhythm—not your exception. With each honest choice, each courageous word, each fair action, you are not just leading—you are building momentum that carries the world forward.

Chapter 10: Intentional Growth and Learning

Intentional growth and learning represent the conscious pursuit of becoming more—more capable, more aware, more aligned with one's purpose. In leadership, growth must be proactive, not reactive. Waiting until circumstances demand change is a recipe for stagnation or failure. Intentionality requires leaders to assess not only what they are learning, but why they are learning it. The 'why' gives learning its depth and direction.

Learning becomes transformational when it is tied to a larger mission. It is not enough to gather information; one must apply it in service of something greater. As a motivational speaker with a background in education and leadership, I've seen that growth often begins with discomfort. We do not grow in ease; we grow in friction. Schools, businesses, and communities thrive when their leaders embrace learning as a lifelong endeavor, rather than a stage of life limited to youth or formal education.

Intentional learning is about quality, not just quantity. Reading a hundred books means little without reflection, application, and integration. Leaders must model intellectual humility. Admitting what you don't know is the first step toward discovering what you need to know. When growth is intentional, learning plans become part of the strategic vision.

Development is tracked, evaluated, and celebrated—not left to chance. In every setting I've led—from classrooms to board-rooms—those who grow the most are those who embrace the process, not just the results. Intentional growth is not about waiting for opportunity—it is about preparing for it. Leaders must build capacity before the call comes. A growth mindset requires embracing feedback not as criticism, but as guidance.

The most transformative leaders seek it out rather than shy away from it. Learning through reflection is just as important as learning through action. Time spent evaluating successes and failures unlocks wisdom. In education, we teach students to set goals and measure progress. That same principle must apply to adult learners and professionals who seek mastery.

Technology and innovation have made knowledge more accessible than ever. The challenge is not in finding information, but in curating meaningful learning experiences. As a school principal, I encouraged staff to pursue professional development with purpose. The most effective educators weren't the ones who attended the most work-shops—but those who implemented their learning with fidelity. In community leadership, intentional growth includes cultural aware-ness and active listening.

To serve a diverse population well, one must continually learn about it. The most effective growth plans are holistic. They address intellectual, emotional, physical, and spiritual development—because leadership flows from the whole person. It is a myth that experience alone leads to growth. Experience plus reflection and intention creates transformation.

Even in adversity, learning is possible. Some of my most valuable lessons came from seasons of uncertainty—because those moments forced me to stretch beyond what was comfortable. True learning is both active and reflective. It happens when we engage with new ideas and take time to internalize what they mean for our work and our world. As professionals, our credibility is tied to our capacity for growth.

People trust leaders who are willing to evolve in the face of new data, shifting needs, and unexpected challenges. A growth-oriented leader is not afraid to revisit assumptions. They challenge their own thinking as often as they challenge the systems around them. One of the most intentional practices in my leadership journey was journaling. Documenting my decisions, mistakes, and insights helped me see patterns I would have otherwise missed.

Learning should be customized. Just as differentiated instruction serves students best, differentiated professional learning respects the unique strengths and gaps of each leader. Strategic learning aligns with purpose. When growth activities are rooted in core values and organizational mission, they gain traction and relevance. Growth requires grit.

There are seasons where improvement is slow or invisible—but in those times, perseverance is the indicator of progress. Learning environments matter. Whether it's a school, office, or community group, people are more likely to grow when they feel safe, supported, and seen. Leaders must champion learning in public. Sharing what we're reading, discussing what we're exploring, and acknowledging what we're still learning gives others permission to do the same.

Mentorship is one of the most powerful tools for intentional learning. A mentor doesn't just teach—they challenge, encourage, and walk alongside you in growth. Learning is not a destination but a lifelong journey. It is the consistent pursuit of new perspectives, improved practices, and deeper understanding. Intentional growth requires prioritization.

Leaders must carve out time and space for learning—because if growth is optional, it will always be postponed. Professional development should never be confined to a checklist. The best learning is immersive, reflective, and directly tied to one's passions and purpose. Some of the most impactful growth experiences happen outside the traditional training sessions—in hallway conversations, late-night reflections, or moments of failure. In my experience as a school leader, intentional growth occurred when teachers collaborated across departments, blending insights from math, literature, and the arts to inspire new instruction.

Growth and learning are inherently relational. Dialogue with others challenges our assumptions and strengthens our clarity. Curiosity is the root of growth. When leaders stop asking questions, they begin to stagnate. Questions keep us connected to the needs around us and the knowledge within reach.

It is not enough to consume content; we must also create it. Writing, speaking, and teaching are powerful forms of learning that force us to synthesize and clarify our thoughts. As technology evolves, so must our learning strategies. Being intentional means adapting to the tools and environments where growth can be amplified. Growth is not always linear.

Sometimes we revisit lessons we thought we had mastered. These returns are not failures—they are deepening of wisdom and perspective. Leadership without learning is directionless. Every new initiative, every policy shift, requires a mindset that is open and ready to grow. The culture of an organization is deeply influenced by its leader's commitment to growth.

A learning leader cultivates a learning team. Growth should be measured not just by what one knows but by how that knowledge shapes behavior and decision-making. The most dangerous phrase in any organization is, 'We've always done it this way.' Intentional growth dares to ask, 'What if there's a better way?' In today's world, adaptability is a leadership superpower—and it is born out of consistent, intentional learning. Time spent on development is not a luxury—it's a necessity. Leaders must see it as an investment in the future, not a detour from the present.

Learning requires unlearning. Sometimes we must dismantle outdated beliefs, strategies, or habits to make room for new, more effective ones. When I coached aspiring leaders, I always emphasized the importance of learning in community. Growth accelerates when it's shared and supported. In every sector—from education to corporate leadership—those who lead best are those who never stop being students.

Ultimately, intentional growth is an act of service. As we grow, we expand our capacity to lead, to connect, and to positively impact others. Leaders must constantly recalibrate their perspectives. What worked yesterday might not work tomorrow, and growth means staying ahead of that curve. When you cultivate a mindset of lifelong learning, you start to see challenges as opportunities rather than setbacks.

The best leaders are not necessarily the most experienced, but the most teachable. Teachability keeps the mind open, the ego in check, and the mission in focus. In the classroom and beyond, intentional learning requires a balance of discipline and curiosity—knowing when to dig deep and when to explore widely. One of the most powerful questions a leader can ask is, 'What am I not seeing?' This invites feedback, collaboration, and ultimately, stronger outcomes. Digital literacy is a modern requirement for intentional growth.

Leaders must stay competent in the tools that shape communication, collaboration, and data-driven decision-making. True professional development shifts from knowing to doing. Application is where insight becomes impact. Reading widely—from leadership texts to biographies to fiction—expands not just knowledge, but empathy and critical thinking. To grow intentionally, leaders must seek tension—not to cause conflict, but to uncover truth.

It's often in uncomfortable conversations that the greatest learning occurs. A true growth mindset embraces revision. Whether in writing, planning, or leading, the ability to rework and improve is a hallmark of maturity. Intentional growth also requires leaders to stay rooted in purpose. Without clarity of why one is learning, even the best efforts may become scattered or misdirected.

Just as organizations need strategic plans, individuals need learning plans—clear objectives, measurable progress markers, and aligned resources. We cannot talk about intentional growth without emphasizing emotional intelligence. Learning how to regulate emotions, read a room, and manage stress is just as vital as mastering technical skills. Leaders who prioritize self-awareness grow faster and deeper than those who operate on autopilot. Self-reflection sharpens judgment and refines leadership voice.

Investing in growth communicates value to others. When a leader pursues knowledge, it signals that development is not only allowed but expected across the organization. Growth can be incremental or exponential. The important part is that it is intentional and consistent. Even a small shift, sustained over time, can change a life or a culture.

In team environments, intentional growth creates cohesion. When everyone is committed to learning, trust increases, silos disappear, and creativity flourishes. I've found that public commitments to growth—like announcing a new skill you're working on—create accountability and inspire others to do the same. Leadership conferences and retreats offer condensed moments of high-impact learning. But without follow-up, their benefits often fade.

Integration is key. One of the best ways to reinforce learning is to teach it. When leaders pass on knowledge, they strengthen their own understanding and elevate their teams. In moments of organizational change, the leaders who thrive are those who have been cultivating their skills and mindsets all along. Preparation meets opportunity.

Growth should be celebrated as part of a team's identity. When learning becomes a value, it naturally shapes how people approach their roles and responsibilities. Feedback loops must be designed into leadership systems. Learning without feedback is like sailing without a compass—directionless and inefficient. One powerful strategy for intentional learning is backward mapping—starting with where you want to go and determining the knowledge and experiences needed to get there.

Professional learning should also include cross-sector exploration. Sometimes, the most innovative ideas come from outside one's immediate field. Learning is most effective when it is relevant and timely. Leaders must be agile enough to adapt their learning goals based on real-time challenges and opportunities. Intentional growth also means growing others.

Leaders multiply their impact when they cultivate leadership capacity in those around them. Reflection is not just for the end of the day. Intentional leaders build it into their routines—after meetings, before decisions, and during conversations. Technology can accelerate growth, but it should not replace the human elements of mentorship, dialogue, and lived experience. In my community work, I've seen how adult learners blossom when they are treated as partners in learning, rather than passive recipients of information.

The pursuit of growth is also the pursuit of excellence. It's not about perfection—it's about improving step by step, day by day. Learning must be proactive, not reactive. Waiting for a crisis to build capacity is the mark of a stagnant organization. Leaders who commit to intentional learning often serve as catalysts within their systems.

Their momentum encourages others to stretch and reach. Incorporating self-assessments and leadership inventories helps leaders identify blind spots and set targeted goals for growth. A powerful but underused learning tool is storytelling. Reflecting on real leadership experiences—and hearing the stories of others—creates lasting lessons. Intentional growth allows leaders to adapt across contexts.

The best principles transfer between sectors, industries, and even generations. Peer learning groups provide mutual accountability and insight. It's in shared reflection that clarity and courage often emerge. The most dangerous kind of stagnation is quiet. It looks like productivity, but beneath the surface, growth has ceased.

As a principal, I learned to treat every professional development day as sacred space—an opportunity to empower, reframe, and reignite the hearts of my staff. When learning is aligned with service, its impact multiplies. The more we grow, the more we can give—to our students, our communities, and our teams. Strategic growth is anchored in purpose, not pressure. Leaders who grow out of a sense of mission are more grounded and resilient than those who grow out of fear or competition.

Journaling is one of the most overlooked leadership tools. The act of writing thoughts, questions, and goals clarifies thinking and tracks evolution. Mentorship fosters growth that books and videos alone cannot. It is in the exchange of experience and encouragement that transformation often occurs. Not every learning opportunity needs a formal setting.

Coffee chats, podcasts, and shadowing other professionals can yield powerful insights. Leadership is a dynamic craft. What worked last year may not work today, which is why growth must be intentional and ongoing. Leaders must learn to pause. Silence is not absence—it's space for reflection, vision, and recalibration.

Without it, growth becomes noise. Professional growth is not just about climbing ladders; it's also about going deeper—understanding context, people, and purpose more fully. Even setbacks offer lessons. When analyzed through a growth lens, failure becomes feedback, and feedback becomes the foundation of future strength. Intentional growth changes culture.

It creates an atmosphere of hope, progress, and the belief that better is always possible. As a motivational speaker and educational leader, I've seen that the most impactful growth journeys are those that ripple outward—igniting change beyond the individual and into the collective. Growth is not limited to formal credentials or certificates. Some of the most valuable development occurs through lived experiences and reflective practice. Leaders should not only seek to grow but to evolve—transforming how they think, engage, and respond in real time.

A culture of intentional growth builds psychological safety. It invites people to ask questions, admit mistakes, and pursue improvement without fear. One of the simplest ways to track growth is by revisiting past decisions and reflecting on what you would do differently today. Technology should be leveraged for learning but not worshiped. Critical thinking and human connection must still drive the growth process.

Intentional learners chase understanding, not just information. They look for meaning beneath metrics and context behind content. In my time as a principal, I witnessed that teachers who embraced growth were more confident in the classroom and more collaborative in the staff room. Leadership retreats and reflection days should be scheduled with as much seriousness as performance reviews—they are investments in capacity. Growth invites vulnerability.

It asks us to admit we don't know, to fail in public, and to commit to learning despite discomfort. Ultimately, intentional growth isn't just about personal success—it's about leaving people and places better than we found them. The beauty of growth is that it is self-perpetuating. Once a leader begins evolving intentionally, it creates a hunger to continue learning. Learning how to learn is a skill in itself—knowing what questions to ask, where to look for answers, and how to evaluate credibility.

Reflection should be more than a retrospective glance—it should be a forward-facing tool, shaping tomorrow's goals based on yesterday's insights. Great leaders are not repositories of knowledge but curators of perspective. They organize learning in ways that empower others to think critically. Every interaction can become a lesson. Observing how people respond, lead, or collaborate provides live case studies in leadership development.

Intentional growth honors both speed and stillness—times of acceleration and moments of deliberate pause to consider the bigger picture. We grow when we step outside our comfort zones. Challenges, while uncomfortable, are fertile ground for breakthrough insights. I've encouraged many young professionals to keep a 'leadership journal'—a space for capturing lessons, quotes, breakthroughs, and future aspirations. The more intentional we are about growth, the more equipped we become to guide others on their learning journeys.

A true growth environment makes it unacceptable to remain stagnant. When curiosity is contagious, culture shifts from compliance to innovation. When intentional growth becomes part of a leader's identity, every encounter becomes an opportunity to evolve, inspire, and refine one's craft. Learning is not a seasonal pursuit; it is a daily discipline. Leaders must be as committed to their growth on ordinary days as they are during peak seasons.

In environments where people feel safe to share ideas and take risks, growth accelerates. Fear inhibits learning, while trust ignites it. Collaboration multiplies capacity. When individuals pursue growth collectively, the impact reaches beyond personal development—it transforms communities. There's a difference between learning for performance and learning for purpose.

Leaders who learn for purpose align growth with mission, not just metrics. The practice of debriefing—whether after events, meetings, or challenges—builds a reflective culture that transforms experience into wisdom. Self-directed learning cultivates ownership. When leaders chart their own development path, they engage more deeply and retain more meaningfully. Growth-minded leaders encourage feedback, even when it's hard to hear.

They understand that critique, when offered constructively, is a gift. I recall mentoring a team of educators who designed a growth plan that included book studies, cross-visits to other schools, and action research. The results were staggering—not just in student achievement, but in professional joy. The ultimate goal of intentional growth is not simply to know more—it's to become more. More aware, more capable, more generous, and more impactful.

Growth is a journey of courage. It calls on us to acknowledge what we don't know, to reach for what feels unfamiliar, and to persist even when progress is invisible. Every leader needs a personal growth blueprint. Whether it's through reading, listening, observing, or doing—consistent exposure to new ideas is essential. I've found that intentional learning requires a dual lens: one focused inward for self-awareness and another focused outward for situational understanding.

In fast-paced environments, leaders who grow intentionally learn to pause without losing momentum. They build habits of critical thinking amidst the whirlwind of decisions. Just as athletes train between games, leaders must develop between crises. Preparation breeds clarity when pressure arises. True growth involves wrestling with complexity.

It's about learning to navigate gray areas, ask better questions, and lead with empathy over ego. Sometimes, growth looks like unlearning—releasing outdated mindsets and practices that no longer serve your purpose or your people. Leaders must also grow their capacity to rest. Rejuvenation is a form of learning—it reconnects us with our vision, our energy, and our creativity. As an educator, I integrated reflection journals into my leadership teams—not to grade performance, but to provoke thought and track growth over time.

Growth without direction is noise. Intentional learning must be aligned with purpose, grounded in values, and focused on service to others. When leaders commit to lifelong learning, they demonstrate humility—the acknowledgment that there is always more to understand, more to master, and more to give. Organizational growth mirrors leadership growth. Teams reflect the developmental appetite and mindset of those guiding them.

I once coached a leadership team that embraced quarterly growth challenges—each member committed to a new skill, and the ripple effect was innovation across the campus. Books can broaden the mind, but conversations sharpen it. Dialogue invites critique, comparison, and real-time reflection that deepens understanding. Growth must be contextualized. A strategy that works in one district, industry, or setting must be adapted—not copied—for another.

One of the most powerful questions a leader can ask is, 'What am I missing?' This inquiry opens the door to new information and diverse viewpoints. Clarity and growth are connected. When you define what success looks like, you create a roadmap for intentional development. The greatest evidence of learning is not a certificate, but a shift in behavior—when knowledge moves from theory to consistent action. Intentional growth also involves scaling impact.

Leaders grow not just to improve themselves, but to elevate everyone within their sphere of influence. As a principal, I encouraged my staff to attend conferences not just for information, but to bring back strategies that would transform student experiences. Intentional growth demands consistency. It is not a burst of motivation followed by stagnation, but a deliberate rhythm of renewal and challenge. Learning should be embedded in the leadership schedule—not as an afterthought but as a strategic pillar.

Planning time for development signals its value. The difference between aspiring leaders and effective leaders often lies in the discipline to grow when no one is watching. In every district I've served, the most effective educators were those who remained teachable. Their openness became contagious to students and peers alike. There is no 'finish line' for leadership development.

Mastery is a moving target, and those who lead best are constantly recalibrating their aim. Growth without integrity leads to manipulation. True leadership development must be anchored in authenticity and ethical practice. Workshops and seminars are valuable, but only if participants apply what they've learned. Transformation requires implementation.

Every setback is an invitation to grow. When leaders reframe challenges as lessons, they model resilience for their teams. The best professional learning communities I've witnessed are built on trust, reflection, and shared accountability for improvement. In educational leadership, growth means knowing your students—not just curriculum or policies. It means listening, observing, and adapting to meet real needs.

A culture of growth starts with language. Leaders who speak about possibilities, progress, and perseverance create an atmosphere where learning thrives. Growth is not passive; it is a pursuit. It requires attention, effort, and reflection—not just exposure to new information. It's easy to mistake movement for progress.

Intentional learning ensures that each step is purposeful, each effort aligned with deeper objectives. Even in failure, there is feedback. Wise leaders extract insight from every misstep and share those insights transparently to uplift others. Professional development should not be a checkbox. When personalized and practical, it becomes a source of energy, not obligation.

In my leadership experience, the best growth occurred when people were trusted to lead their own development initiatives and share outcomes. Mentorship accelerates learning. By walking alongside someone more experienced, leaders fast-track their own reflection and receive real-time wisdom. Growth-oriented environments protect time for learning. They treat it as sacred—not squeezed into spare minutes, but intentionally carved into calendars.

To grow means to see further than yesterday. Vision expands when learning deepens; perspective shifts when understanding broadens. Ultimately, intentional growth turns knowledge into influence. It converts insight into impact, ensuring our learning outlives our leadership roles. Leadership growth is both an internal and external process.

It starts with awareness but must translate into behavior others can trust and follow. When I facilitated leadership retreats, we often began with reflection exercises that forced us to examine our personal learning roadmaps and blind spots. Some of the most significant growth happens in the valleys, not the mountaintops. Adversity has a unique way of sharpening focus and strengthening resolve. Intentional growth challenges us to think long-term.

It's not just about solving today's problems, but about preparing for opportunities we haven't yet imagined. True learning is transformative—it should disrupt comfort zones, reframe assumptions, and demand a new level of commitment. Leaders who prioritize growth do so not for recognition, but because they understand their influence multiplies when they are continually evolving. It is not enough to learn. We must also teach.

Sharing knowledge is a powerful reinforcement of personal mastery and a gift to those around us. Personal growth and organizational excellence are inextricably linked. When one rises, the other follows. Learning isn't confined to professional content. Lessons in parenting, wellness, community service, and travel often produce the deepest revelations.

As we grow with intention, we don't just change what we do—we redefine who we are and how we show up in the world. The most impactful leaders are not those who know the most, but those who are always willing to learn more. I once worked with a district leader who made it a point to attend classroom walkthroughs not to evaluate, but to learn from teachers and students alike. Growth is deeply personal. What stretches one leader may comfort another, so intentional development must be tailored to the learner's stage and setting.

Great organizations grow because their people grow. They prioritize learning as part of the culture—not just an initiative, but an identity. One of my favorite practices is to end every day by journaling one new insight. Over time, these notes become a mosaic of progress and potential. Curiosity fuels growth.

Leaders who ask more questions than they give answers cultivate innovation in themselves and in their teams. Continuous learning is the bridge between today's problems and tomorrow's solutions. It's how we stay relevant and responsive in changing times. Feedback loops are essential. Leaders who actively seek input from peers, staff, and even students build a holistic view of their impact.

During my tenure as a principal, the most transformative moments came from listening circles where all voices were welcomed and valued. To be intentional about learning is to be intentional about legacy. Every skill gained, every lesson embraced contributes to the blueprint we leave behind. The best leaders don't just embrace change—they chase growth with urgency and clarity, knowing the future favors the prepared. When I reflect on the schools I've led, the turning points always came when staff aligned their personal growth goals with student-centered outcomes.

Intentional learning means holding space for reflection. It's in those quiet moments of introspection that deep shifts occur. In leadership, you're either growing or you're becoming obsolete. The pace of the world demands proactive, not reactive, development. One of the keys to sustainable growth is pacing.

Leaders must balance intensity with longevity—stretching without snapping. I've coached emerging leaders to build what I call 'learning ecosystems'—deliberate environments filled with feedback, modeling, and diverse perspectives. The classroom is still my greatest teacher. Every student interaction has the potential to teach humility, perspective, and flexibility. There is wisdom in struggle.

When we view setbacks as stepping stones, we reclaim agency and extract lessons that propel us forward. Growth is not about perfection—it's about movement. Every step, even if small, is progress when done with intention. Ultimately, intentional growth empowers legacy. It ensures our leadership lives on through those we've influenced, mentored, and inspired.

A powerful practice I've adopted is conducting monthly 'growth audits'—where I assess what I've learned, where I've improved, and what still needs attention. In education, stagnation is a silent threat. When we stop learning, we risk becoming disconnected from those we aim to lead and serve. The journey of growth is deeply tied to emotional intelligence. Leaders must not only expand their knowledge but their empathy, awareness, and self-control.

A leader's growth impacts generations. The values we sharpen and the skills we refine ripple through classrooms, boardrooms, and communities. I often challenge my mentees to maintain a 'learning ledger'—a running log of lessons learned, questions sparked, and resources explored each week. Leaders must be willing to unlearn outdated habits to make space for new strategies. Growth is as much about release as it is about acquisition.

Real learning ignites when theory meets real-world tension. It's in the friction of application that ideas become wisdom. Personal learning goals should align with leadership purpose. When our why drives our what, growth becomes mission-aligned and motivating. Learning is a service.

When leaders invest in growth, they become more effective in solving problems, lifting others, and stewarding change. The reward of intentional growth is not just knowledge—it's transformation. We become better equipped, more compassionate, and more impactful leaders. The most courageous leaders are those who admit they don't know everything—and then pursue the knowledge to fill that gap. Intentional growth calls for intentional disruption.

Leaders must disrupt their routines to gain new perspectives and deeper insights. I've grown most when I've had to lead through uncertainty. Crisis doesn't just reveal character—it refines it. One strategy that has fueled my development is surrounding myself with people who challenge my thinking, not just echo it. We learn best when we're slightly uncomfortable.

That tension is where resilience is built and breakthroughs are born. Leadership development must include cultural competency. Growth without awareness of context leads to disconnected leadership. When we learn, we light the way. Every insight we gain has the potential to illuminate a path for someone else.

As leaders, we must model what we expect. If we want our teams to grow, they must see us doing the same—consistently and transparently. Every learning moment, no matter how small, adds to a leader's toolbox. Growth is cumulative, and mastery is built brick by brick. The future belongs to the learners.

In a rapidly evolving world, those who remain curious will remain capable. When growth becomes a habit, learning becomes a lifestyle. It seeps into every conversation, every challenge, and every opportunity. I remember a teacher who transformed their classroom after one workshop—not because of the training, but because they made the learning personal. Intentional growth is about choice.

Every day, leaders choose to engage with content, with people, and with purpose to get better. Growth-minded leaders do not fear change—they facilitate it. Their learning drives the innovation their teams need to thrive. Reflection is the bridge between experience and growth. Without it, we repeat lessons instead of building on them.

As a principal, I made time every week to observe, listen, and journal. Those small practices accumulated into transformational insight. There is no finish line to personal growth. There is always another level, another layer, another lesson to uncover. The legacy of a leader is not defined by position, but by progression.

What did they learn? Who did they help grow? The more we grow, the more we understand how much more there is to learn. This humility keeps us grounded and hungry for impact. To lead with intention is to grow with purpose.

And in that journey, we don't just change the world—we become the kind of leaders the world needs most.

Chapter 11: Cultivating Community Impact

Community impact doesn't begin with programs or policies—it begins with people. At the heart of every thriving community is a collective of individuals who believe in investing in one another's growth and wellbeing. As a school principal and community leader, I've seen firsthand how one intentional act can ripple through a neighborhood.

Whether it's a literacy night at a school or a mentorship event at a local park, authentic engagement shifts the community's trajectory. Cultivating community impact requires leaders to step beyond institutional boundaries. It means bringing classrooms to the streets, boardrooms to block parties, and learning to the lives of those often overlooked. True community transformation doesn't come from outside-in; it must be inside-out. Those most affected by decisions must be empowered to help shape them.

In my years of educational leadership, one of the most powerful community partnerships began with a listening session—no presentations, no agendas—just open ears and open hearts. When people feel seen, heard, and valued, they invest. This is the cornerstone of sustainable community development: dignity and trust. Impact is not measured by headlines or hashtags, but by the quiet progress of lives changed, youth empowered, and cycles of poverty disrupted by opportunity. Every school, nonprofit, and faith organization is part of a larger ecosystem.

When we connect our efforts, rather than compete, we multiply our influence. It's not enough to serve the community—we must serve with the community. Collaboration must be mutual, not paternalistic. Leadership that cultivates community impact is humble, consistent, and anchored in service. It looks for long-term change, not quick wins.

Community impact thrives when leadership prioritizes presence over perfection. Being available to listen, collaborate, and adapt shows authenticity. I've learned that consistent engagement, not just episodic programming, builds the kind of trust that can withstand challenges and drive progress. In one of my former schools, we launched a community garden initiative that brought parents, students, and local farmers together. It became more than just a food project—it was a symbol of shared investment in our youth.

Impact must be both visible and measurable. While relationships are foundational, the outcomes must reflect tangible progress in education, economic mobility, and social equity. Civic partnerships are most effective when roles are clearly defined and mutual accountability is established. Every stakeholder should know how their contribution supports the collective mission. We cannot overlook the power of storytelling.

When community members share their narratives, they humanize the data and inspire deeper commitment to change. The schools that succeed in community engagement often have liaisons or coordinators dedicated to relationship-building. This intentional role elevates the importance of communication and continuity. Leadership must also be fluent in the language of advocacy. Sometimes the most significant impact comes from using influence to amplify unheard voices at decision-making tables.

One of the greatest gifts a leader can offer a community is capacity-building. It's not just about doing for people, but equipping them to lead themselves. True community impact recognizes the diversity of experiences and needs. Equity must be embedded in every initiative, ensuring resources meet people where they are. Every leader should ask themselves: What legacy are we leaving in the communities we serve?

Impact without continuity is merely a moment, but sustainable change builds momentum. Our greatest measure of success isn't the size of our outreach, but the depth of our relationships. A few well-nurtured partnerships can yield more than dozens of shallow connections. Community engagement is a leadership discipline. It must be learned, practiced, and evaluated with the same intensity as academic or operational goals.

When communities see leaders who are consistent and accountable, trust is strengthened. And when trust is strengthened, cooperation flourishes. It's important to honor the culture of a community, not try to overwrite it. Impactful leaders study, respect, and uplift the history, values, and identity of the people they serve. One initiative that brought lasting change was a monthly open forum where residents and school officials met to co-create solutions.

Ideas ranged from after-school tutoring to neighborhood cleanups—and all came from listening first. Leaders must stop asking what's wrong with communities and start asking what's strong in them. This asset-based lens allows us to build from strength, not just respond to deficit. We cannot build community with drive-by relationships. Showing up regularly, with no agenda other than connection, is where credibility is earned.

Schools and civic groups must become beacons of hope, not just centers of service. The tone we set affects how community members see their own power and potential. Collaboration is not about compromise—it's about co-ownership. When communities co-own the vision, they will co-create the future. I've learned that community impact isn't about being the loudest voice in the room—it's about being the one who listens the most.

When leaders make room for grassroots wisdom, they uncover innovative solutions that can't be taught in any textbook or boardroom. Too often, systems are built for efficiency, not equity. But true community impact demands we center justice, ensuring that everyone has access and opportunity. Community isn't built on programs alone; it's forged in shared experiences, mutual respect, and collective dreams. An effective leader becomes a cultural translator—helping diverse groups understand one another and collaborate despite differences in background or belief.

Many of the most impactful community projects I've witnessed started with a simple question: What do you need most right now? Empowering local youth to lead community initiatives not only develops future leaders but also ensures that projects resonate with the lived experiences of those they aim to serve. Data can guide decisions, but stories drive them. When we share the real lives behind the statistics, hearts and minds shift in powerful ways. We must remember that buildings and budgets are tools—not goals.

The true purpose of leadership is to improve lives and expand access to opportunity. Impactful community leadership isn't about fixing people—it's about walking with them, supporting their agency, and honoring their wisdom. In one neighborhood revitalization project I participated in, the most important contribution didn't come from an elected official or nonprofit—it came from a grandmother who organized block watch meetings and weekly youth lunches. Her presence became the soul of the project. Community impact is sustainable when it is embedded into daily rhythms, not reserved for annual events.

Ongoing relationship-building outpaces episodic involvement every time. Leaders must also learn to share the spotlight. Empowering others to lead doesn't diminish authority—it multiplies influence. When schools open their doors to the community after hours—for workshops, dinners, and celebrations—they become trusted hubs of hope and connection. Success is not measured in the number of initiatives launched, but in the number of lives changed.

One life transformed can uplift a family, a block, even a generation. We can't build strong communities without strong stories. Capturing and sharing the journeys of local heroes—unsung educators, caregivers, youth leaders—gives others permission to dream and lead. Restorative practices, such as community circles and healing dialogues, should be as common in neighborhoods as they are in progressive classrooms. They cultivate understanding, repair harm, and build social capital.

When people feel that their voices matter, they begin to show up not just to be heard, but to help lead. Civic participation grows in the soil of dignity. Effective leaders in community spaces practice radical empathy—they don't just sympathize with pain, they commit to solutions with those experiencing it. Every community challenge carries with it the seeds of its own solution. Leaders cultivate impact by creating the conditions for those seeds to grow.

Building community impact requires a long-game mindset. Real transformation doesn't happen in a single school year or grant cycle—it unfolds over years of faithful investment and iterative learning. Faith-based institutions often serve as vital anchors in communities. Partnering with churches, mosques, and temples opens doors to trust, cultural knowledge, and grassroots mobilization. Community impact means putting resources where people are, not expecting people to come to the resources.

Mobile food pantries, sidewalk tutoring, and neighborhood listening tours bring services to the doorsteps of need. We must normalize celebration. Honoring community wins—big or small—reinforces hope and invites continued engagement. Too often, we rush past success without pausing to reflect and rejoice. Intentional design of public spaces can also influence impact.

A well-lit park or colorful mural may seem simple, but they communicate safety, pride, and creativity. The environment shapes the emotional tone of the neighborhood. Sometimes, the most powerful move a leader can make is to step back. Creating space for others to take initiative, even if imperfectly, reinforces shared ownership of progress. Youth advisory boards have become one of the most effective tools in my leadership toolkit.

When we empower students to shape school policy or civic projects, they show us just how much capacity and insight they already hold. Digital tools can also extend community impact. Social media campaigns, virtual town halls, and SMS alerts make connection and collaboration possible even beyond in-person interaction. Crisis moments reveal the strength—or fragility—of our community infrastructure. When COVID-19 hit, communities with pre-existing networks of trust mobilized faster and served more equitably.

One of the most profound truths about community work is this: we do not serve to be thanked, we serve because it's who we are. Servant leadership is the soul of community transformation. Mentorship is another powerful lever for cultivating community impact. When adults invest time mentoring youth, the ripple effect touches families, schools, and even future workplaces. It's important to dismantle the myth that only big initiatives create change.

Sometimes, a reading circle, a community cookout, or a youth-led art show can awaken a new spirit of pride and collaboration. Data-informed decision-making helps leaders identify gaps in service, assess community needs, and prioritize impact. However, numbers should guide—not dictate—the narrative. Human stories must always accompany data. Communities thrive when education is integrated into everyday life.

Parent education nights, financial literacy workshops, and intergenerational learning sessions build collective capacity. In one collaboration, we co-designed a parent leadership institute that trained local caregivers to advocate for better policies, navigate the school system, and lead their own neighborhood projects. They became ambassadors of progress. The language we use in community matters. Referring to residents as 'partners' or 'collaborators' instead of 'recipients' affirms dignity and shared agency.

There's a rhythm to impactful engagement: listen, co-create, implement, reflect, and revise. Skipping any step can lead to misalignment and mistrust. When communities are included in evaluation—asking what worked and what didn't—they not only offer insight, they feel seen and respected. Feedback loops should be accessible and transparent. Equity audits are another valuable tool.

They help leaders see blind spots in resource allocation, representation, and policy design—areas that may unintentionally perpetuate disparities. Ultimately, the most lasting community impact is generational. When today's children grow up believing their voice matters, their ideas are valid, and their actions lead to real change, we've succeeded. One of the most powerful models of community impact I've encountered was a neighborhood microgrant initiative. Residents could apply for small amounts of funding to implement their own solutions—ranging from community gardens to elder care programs.

The results far exceeded what any top-down program could achieve. To cultivate lasting change, leaders must also focus on succession planning. Community impact is diminished when it is tied solely to one person's charisma or tenure. Empowering emerging leaders to carry the torch ensures sustainability. Celebrating diversity within a community requires more than token gestures.

True inclusion means elevating voices that have historically been marginalized and making space for their narratives to shape the future. We must resist the urge to always be the problem-solvers. Sometimes, the most meaningful support is showing up, holding space, and simply saying, 'I believe in you.' It's important to remember that communities are not monolithic. They consist of overlapping identities, needs, and histories.

Leaders must engage with humility and a commitment to ongoing learning. Cross-sector partnerships are critical to community impact. When schools, local businesses, health providers, and nonprofits align their efforts, the outcomes multiply exponentially. Cultural events—parades, festivals, heritage celebrations—are not just entertainment. They are vital opportunities for storytelling, healing, and belonging.

Youth empowerment should not be limited to extracurriculars. Young people should be at the table when discussing issues that affect their neighborhoods—from public safety to environmental justice. Accessibility must be a non-negotiable part of community engagement. Events should offer translation services, childcare, transportation support, and accommodations for disabilities to ensure full participation. As I reflect on years of service, one truth rises above the rest: change doesn't happen to communities—it happens with them.

That partnership is where true impact begins. One of the overlooked strategies for community development is asset mapping. Instead of focusing on deficiencies, asset mapping identifies the talents, skills, and resources already present within a community. This approach energizes rather than discourages. Community impact is often catalyzed by simple, relational acts.

A principal who greets students by name at the door, a store owner who hires neighborhood teens, or a coach who mentors off the field—all of these contribute to the invisible scaffolding of trust and safety. Effective community leaders are bridge builders. They listen to concerns, translate them into shared language, and help diverse groups work toward common goals, even when priorities differ. Storytelling events such as oral history nights or podcast projects can deepen empathy across generations. Hearing firsthand accounts of triumph and hardship creates a powerful human connection.

One of the most meaningful community projects I've witnessed was a 'Memory Wall' where residents could write messages to honor lost loved ones and celebrate personal milestones. It became a sacred space of grief, gratitude, and healing. Investing in community leadership pipelines changes the trajectory of neighborhoods. Programs that train and mentor local residents to run for office, lead PTAs, or launch nonprofits create a cycle of empowered advocacy. Food justice is a powerful entry point for community impact.

Teaching families to grow their own food, building farmer's markets, and addressing food deserts improves both health and autonomy. Restoring abandoned spaces into community centers, innovation hubs, or youth programs transforms eyesores into beacons. Every neighborhood has potential waiting to be uncovered. Sometimes we have to redefine success. In some communities, progress may mean fewer suspensions, more kids walking to school safely, or a single mother starting her own business.

These wins matter deeply. Above all, community impact requires consistency. Show up. Show up again. And when no one else does—show up anyway.

That's where the magic lives. Volunteerism continues to be a bedrock of meaningful community advancement. Whether it's coaching youth sports, organizing cleanup days, or hosting skills workshops, volunteers embody the spirit of shared responsibility. Many communities benefit from intergenerational programs where older adults mentor youth while also learning new skills from them. These exchanges bridge age gaps and foster mutual respect and curiosity.

Small business development must be prioritized in community revitalization. Supporting entrepreneurs with microloans, mentorship, and co-working spaces seeds economic independence and keeps dollars local. Art is more than aesthetics—it's a tool for reflection and resistance. Murals, spoken word, music, and sculpture give voice to identity and challenge systems of injustice while beautifying public spaces. One successful project I led involved transforming a vacant lot into a pop-up learning park with outdoor classrooms, rotating workshops, and peer-tutoring corners.

It reimagined what learning could look like in underserved areas. To achieve deep impact, community leaders must develop cultural fluency. Understanding the values, languages, and traditions of those we serve allows us to lead with empathy and relevance. Social-emotional learning doesn't stop with children. Community programming that builds emotional intelligence, conflict resolution, and stress management supports collective resilience.

Partnerships with local media amplify community voices. Radio segments, neighborhood newsletters, and public access television can spotlight local heroes and initiatives that deserve attention. Time banking is another emerging strategy in equitable communities. Residents exchange services—like tutoring for car repair—without money changing hands, affirming each person's value. Finally, cultivating community impact means nurturing hope.

In places battered by poverty, crime, or disinvestment, leaders must paint a compelling vision of what's possible and walk with people toward that future. In community work, celebration is strategy. Too often we wait for perfection before recognizing progress. Celebrating incremental wins—like increased parent participation or the launch of a local initiative—motivates continued involvement. Building community trust often begins with consistency and humility.

People don't care what you know until they know that you care. Reliability over time builds the foundation for transformative partnerships. Local libraries, often overlooked, can be reimagined as hubs for civic engagement, digital literacy, and workforce readiness. Community partnerships can extend their services far beyond bookshelves. Civic education is an essential component of community empowerment.

When residents understand how decisions are made—from school board meetings to zoning laws—they're more likely to get involved and advocate effectively. Pop-up community cafes or mobile listening booths have been used to gather community input in low-pressure environments. These formats make participation more accessible and capture honest, diverse perspectives. Environmental stewardship is also community impact. Teaching youth how to test water quality or lead recycling drives cultivates pride in place and habits of responsibility.

Faith-based organizations remain vital allies. Their longstanding community presence, infrastructure, and values make them natural collaborators in efforts around food security, housing, and youth engagement. Mobile services—such as health clinics, job fairs, or legal aid—can reach populations that are otherwise isolated by geography or transportation barriers. These efforts remove access barriers and build trust. Leadership in community is not just about charisma; it's about credibility, compassion, and commitment.

The most effective leaders are those who listen well, act boldly, and stay anchored in purpose. Lastly, never underestimate the ripple effect. A single scholarship fund, mentorship lunch, or youth performance can inspire dozens more efforts. Impact spreads through example. One of the key strategies for cultivating impact is aligning community goals with local government initiatives.

When grassroots efforts sync with public policy, the results are more sustainable and better resourced. Data-driven community engagement ensures that resources are going where they're most needed. Conducting neighborhood surveys, focus groups, and participatory budgeting builds transparency and efficacy. The arts can be a powerful bridge between cultures. Multilingual performances, visual art collaborations, and intercultural festivals help residents appreciate their differences while celebrating shared humanity.

Leaders must remember that not all community members will come to them—sometimes leadership requires going to the people. House visits, block parties, and informal gatherings often build more trust than formal events. One unforgettable initiative I witnessed was a 'Dream Wall,' where community members posted their hopes for the neighborhood. The exercise not only inspired but guided future development priorities based on real dreams. Fostering youth entrepreneurship builds both skills and confidence.

Whether through pop-up shops, digital design, or neighborhood services, young people learn initiative, resilience, and the power of ownership. Mental health support is foundational to sustainable community development. Programs that normalize therapy, provide trauma care, and train mental health first responders allow individuals to flourish and support others. Digital equity has become essential. Free Wi-Fi zones, technology lending libraries, and digital literacy workshops ensure that all community members can access resources, learning, and opportunity.

Neighborhood storytelling projects, like photovoice exhibits or video documentaries, humanize data and preserve legacy. They give voice to lived experience in a way statistics cannot capture. A lasting community impact is never just about today—it's about preparing the ground for tomorrow. Leaders must plant seeds knowing they may not sit under the shade of the trees they've nurtured. Resilient communities are often those where people feel safe enough to share hard truths.

Hosting facilitated dialogues on race, income inequality, education, or public safety invites honesty and builds bridges for long-term healing. Place-making is a concept rooted in community empowerment. It's about transforming physical spaces—parks, intersections, sidewalks—into places where people feel they belong and are proud to gather. The intersection of education and community impact is often overlooked. Schools that open their doors for evening programming, parent education, and job training serve as powerful engines of transformation.

Emergency preparedness is a community responsibility. Training residents in first aid, CPR, and emergency planning fosters resilience in times of natural disasters or public crises. Access to affordable child care is one of the greatest levers for family stability and upward mobility. Community partnerships with local providers and faith institutions can close the gap in availability. Celebrating heritage is vital.

Cultural festivals, oral history projects, and elder interviews validate identity and create intergenerational understanding, strengthening social cohesion. Economic justice must be part of any long-term impact strategy. Advocating for living wages, equitable hiring practices, and small business protections ensures that progress lifts everyone, not just a few. Public transportation can't be ignored. Routes that serve job centers, schools, and grocery stores create economic and social mobility.

Leaders should advocate for safe, frequent, and affordable transit options. Mentoring programs remain one of the most effective tools for long-term change. When youth are paired with committed adults who listen, guide, and believe in them, entire trajectories shift. Community impact begins at the level of relationships. It's not policies alone, but people showing up with consistency, integrity, and heart, that turn neighborhoods into thriving ecosystems of hope.

Access to nutritious food is a cornerstone of community health. Urban agriculture programs, community-supported agriculture (CSA), and mobile produce markets bring healthy options directly to underserved areas. Inclusive recreation is essential for community vitality. Public spaces and programs should welcome people of all ages, abilities, and backgrounds. Playgrounds, walking trails, and fitness zones foster both health and connection.

Youth voice must be integrated into decision-making processes. Advisory boards, youth town halls, and student-led initiatives teach leadership and affirm that young people are essential stakeholders in their community. Financial literacy can be a generational game changer. Offering workshops on budgeting, credit, taxes, and entrepreneurship empowers residents to make informed decisions that impact their long-term stability. Clean and safe neighborhoods require collaboration between residents, law enforcement, local government, and advocacy groups.

Community policing and neighborhood watches help restore accountability and mutual respect. The arts provide a language for healing. Music therapy sessions, poetry circles, and expressive art spaces help people process trauma, find joy, and express identities often suppressed in conventional discourse. One overlooked source of community strength is storytelling. Creating podcasts, community archives, or digital storytelling labs allows residents to reclaim narratives and shape how their neighborhoods are perceived.

Partnerships with higher education institutions can amplify community efforts. Service-learning, research collaborations, and pipeline programs give students real-world experience and communities additional resources. Community impact is magnified when residents become civic leaders. Hosting local leadership academies that train citizens in policy, budgeting, and advocacy can create a groundswell of informed, effective changemakers. Ultimately, the heartbeat of every thriving community is shared responsibility.

When neighbors shift from 'me' to 'we,' transformation takes root and the future becomes a shared masterpiece. Accessible public art tells the story of a community's soul. Murals, sculptures, and street art that reflect the history and hopes of residents foster pride and cultural continuity. Time banks and mutual aid networks have reemerged as powerful tools for grassroots economic exchange. These systems rely on trust and reciprocity, proving that communities can thrive without conventional currency.

Community land trusts are long-term solutions to gentrification and displacement. By holding land in collective ownership, they ensure housing remains affordable and rooted in the interests of local people. Libraries can double as innovation labs. With makerspaces, coding clubs, and career services, they've become digital empowerment centers offering opportunity in unexpected places. Language justice matters.

Offering interpretation, translation, and bilingual signage ensures that all residents—not just English speakers—can participate fully in civic life. Recovery from community trauma requires intentional investments in mental health, education, and public space. Healing circles, community resilience teams, and memorial installations offer pathways to renewal. Civic technology tools—like neighborhood apps, SMS surveys, and online suggestion boards—allow residents to participate in planning and decision-making even if they can't attend in-person meetings. Creative placemaking blends art, activism, and urban design to build identity and foster inclusion.

These efforts transform overlooked spaces into landmarks of memory and aspiration. Sustainability should be woven into every community initiative. Whether through solar installations, green roofs, or waste reduction campaigns, environmental stewardship protects future generations. Leaders who prioritize relationships over recognition build deeper, more lasting community impact. When the spotlight is shared, the movement grows stronger than any one individual.

Shared community rituals—like annual parades, neighborhood cookouts, and cultural celebrations—forge deep connections across generations and reinforce a sense of belonging. Faith-based organizations remain critical pillars in many communities. Their roles extend beyond spiritual care, offering food pantries, counseling, shelter, and social services with trust already built-in. Leadership pipelines within the community ensure that tomorrow's changemakers are prepared today. Programs that identify, mentor, and support emerging leaders help sustain progress long-term.

Civic engagement education should begin early. When students learn about government, advocacy, and community organizing in school, they're better equipped to participate as informed citizens. Neighborhood resilience depends on everyday heroes—block captains, crossing guards, after-school volunteers—who model what it means to care without fanfare. Community journalism plays a vital role in shaping public dialogue. When local stories are told with nuance and integrity, residents feel seen, and important issues are brought to light.

Effective coalitions bring diverse stakeholders together under a common vision. Nonprofits, government agencies, businesses, and residents must all have a seat at the table to ensure equitable solutions. Greening efforts—like tree planting, rain gardens, and community composting—beautify spaces and contribute to environmental health, improving air quality and community morale simultaneously. Digital storytelling workshops empower community members to reclaim their narratives using video, photography, and social media, ensuring stories are preserved in modern formats. Ultimately, cultivating community impact is about legacy.

It's about building a foundation where the next generation has more opportunity, deeper connection, and a clear sense of their collective power. Collaborative grant writing workshops can help small organizations gain access to funding. By sharing resources, expertise, and strategies, communities can unlock external support that may otherwise remain out of reach. Senior citizens possess a wealth of knowledge and experience. Intergenerational programs that pair seniors with youth foster mutual understanding, reduce isolation, and cultivate respect across age groups.

Public health outreach, when led by community members, builds trust and effectiveness. Culturally responsive health fairs, screenings, and vaccine drives save lives and reduce disparities. Celebrating small wins energizes communities. Recognizing a new mural, the opening of a local café, or a successful cleanup day keeps momentum going and encourages ongoing participation. Entrepreneurial ecosystems thrive in communities that support local ideas.

Incubators, pitch nights, and microloans can help residents turn skills into sustainable ventures that enrich the local economy. Community feedback loops are crucial. Whether through surveys, listening sessions, or digital polls, regularly checking in with residents ensures initiatives remain relevant and responsive. Fostering a shared vision means addressing difficult truths. Open dialogue about racism, classism, or displacement must accompany any serious effort to build a better future.

Language matters in shaping narratives. Communities that refer to themselves as 'thriving,' 'resilient,' or 'emerging' rather than 'at-risk' or 'underserved' begin to shift both perception and possibility. Reentry support for formerly incarcerated individuals reduces recidivism and strengthens families. Housing access, job training, and mentorship help restore dignity and create second chances. At its core, community impact is an act of love—a collective expression that says everyone matters, everyone belongs, and together, we can create a future worth inheriting.

Mobile resource centers provide vital services directly to neighborhoods. Equipped with Wi-Fi, job assistance, legal aid, and wellness services, they bring hope and support to where it's needed most. Volunteerism builds both community and character. When families, schools, and businesses prioritize giving back, a culture of shared responsibility and civic pride flourishes. Neighborhood beautification projects—from planting gardens to painting fences—promote ownership, reduce crime, and create spaces where people want to live and gather.

Community members should be recognized as experts in their own lives. Professional planners, developers, and service providers must treat residents not as subjects of aid but as architects of solutions. Digital equity is a justice issue. Expanding internet access, providing technology training, and closing the digital divide ensures all community members can learn, work, and thrive in today's world. Community resilience is rooted in relationships.

When people know and trust their neighbors, they can rely on one another during crises, from natural disasters to economic downturns. Inclusive festivals that honor diverse cultures and heritages help dismantle stereotypes and foster appreciation for the rich mosaic of community life. Pop-up community engagement events—such as mobile town halls or sidewalk suggestion stations—bring local government closer to the people and increase civic participation. Skillsharing workshops empower residents to learn from one another, reinforcing the idea that everyone has something valuable to contribute. Celebrating community milestones, such as the anniversary of a local nonprofit or the opening of a community garden, cultivates a sense of collective achievement and progress.

Mentorship circles are powerful engines for growth. When seasoned professionals, civic leaders, and experienced volunteers share time and wisdom with aspiring changemakers, the entire community evolves. Communities that embrace restorative justice create spaces for healing and accountability. When harm occurs, facilitated conversations and inclusive decision-making can rebuild trust. Local storytelling nights—where residents share personal narratives—strengthen emotional bonds and ensure that history is preserved through the voices of those who lived it.

Impact is best measured not just in statistics, but in stories. A child who finds confidence through a youth theater program, or a senior who reconnects with purpose through a volunteer project, exemplifies community transformation. When people feel seen, heard, and valued, they show up. They contribute. They lead.

Cultivating community impact is not a one-time event but a sustained, intentional lifestyle of care and contribution.

Chapter 12: Legacy Through Service

Legacy is not simply what we leave behind; it is the footprint we create through a life of intentional service. Every act of compassion, every decision made in service to others, builds the narrative of our life's contribution. Those who choose to lead through service often do so without fanfare.

They understand that the truest form of leadership emerges not from titles or accolades, but from a deep-seated commitment to elevate others. Service-driven leaders prioritize people over prestige. They are guided by empathy, fueled by purpose, and anchored in the belief that communities flourish when individuals invest their talents selflessly. Whether mentoring youth, supporting a local nonprofit, or organizing a neighborhood clean-up, the opportunities to create lasting impact are limitless when our motivation stems from service. Educators, for example, shape legacies daily.

A kind word to a struggling student or an after-school tutoring session often plants seeds that flourish years later. These moments, though small in appearance, are monumental in their ripple effect. Similarly, civic leaders who center service in their decision-making processes become stewards of trust. They model integrity, inclusivity, and a long-term vision for their communities, leaving behind systems that uplift generations. True service transcends profession.

A doctor offering pro bono care, an artist leading free community workshops, or a business owner investing in local youth employment—each contributes uniquely to the communal legacy. Legacy through service is an ongoing dialogue between who we are and who we help others become. It is the realization that our greatest influence may not be what we accomplish, but what we empower others to achieve. Service invites reflection. It asks us to consider the needs of our neighbors, to see beyond ourselves, and to commit to action that benefits others—knowing full well that the greatest returns are often unseen and immeasurable.

To build a legacy of service requires consistency. It is forged not in grand gestures alone, but in the cumulative power of showing up, giving generously, and believing in the inherent value of every person we encounter. A legacy of service often begins with a single choice—the choice to see others not as burdens, but as opportunities for connection and contribution. When leaders make this shift, they model a transformative path forward. In educational environments, service-minded administrators foster cultures where student success is measured not just by test scores, but by compassion, equity, and access to opportunity.

These environments leave lasting impressions on students' lives. Principals who serve their staff as instructional coaches, emotional support systems, and community liaisons go beyond traditional roles. They create environments where everyone feels seen, valued, and empowered to lead. Community leaders build legacy through presence. Attending local events, engaging in tough conversations, and listening deeply to the needs of constituents demonstrate service in action and build relational trust.

Every act of service adds to a larger narrative. A legacy is not defined by perfection but by a persistent willingness to show up, adapt, and act in alignment with a higher purpose. Mentorship is one of the most powerful vehicles for legacy building. When seasoned professionals invest in emerging leaders, they extend their influence across generations and industries. Service leadership often requires sacrifice—time, energy, and comfort are willingly exchanged for the greater good.

Yet this sacrifice is not loss; it is investment in the community's future vitality. Nonprofit organizations exemplify legacy through service by addressing systemic needs with grassroots innovation. The leaders of these organizations often go unrecognized, yet their work shapes policy, opportunity, and well-being at scale. Spiritual and faith-based leaders frequently create enduring legacies through community outreach, emotional healing, and moral leadership. Their service acts as a compass in moments of societal and personal uncertainty.

Service becomes legacy when it is sustained, replicated, and celebrated. Encouraging others to carry forward the torch of service ensures that impact does not end with one individual—it multiplies and matures over time. Service leaders understand that their work is not about being the hero, but about creating space for others to shine. They set the stage for collective success rather than personal spotlight. The most impactful legacies are often those that echo through the lives of others long after the originator has stepped away.

Teachers, coaches, and mentors may never see the full fruit of their influence, but their impact is etched in the actions of those they inspired. Building a legacy through service requires emotional resilience. It means continuing to give, even when recognition is sparse or when results take years to materialize. Social entrepreneurs, driven by service rather than profit, often spark powerful movements. Their ventures meet unfulfilled needs, transform communities, and reimagine what business can look like when guided by purpose.

Legacy is shaped not only by public action but by private integrity. Serving one's family, showing up consistently for loved ones, and nurturing relationships are equally vital threads in the fabric of a life well-lived. Leadership rooted in service becomes magnetic. People are drawn to those who serve with sincerity and humility, who model courage in kindness and power in patience. A service-oriented legacy often begins at home.

Children raised in households where volunteering, generosity, and advocacy are normalized tend to carry forward these values in their own lives. Sometimes, service is quiet. It's checking in on a lonely neighbor, picking up trash no one else sees, or donating anonymously to support a struggling family. These acts may be small in scale but enormous in meaning. Institutions that prioritize service become breeding grounds for future leaders.

When schools, businesses, and governments celebrate volunteerism and civic responsibility, they instill a lifelong ethic of giving back. The ripple effect of service is profound. One kind gesture can inspire a movement. One opportunity offered can launch a career. One listening ear can heal a wound.

These ripples form the legacy we leave in our wake. A service legacy is strengthened when we uplift the unheard. Those who amplify marginalized voices, advocate for justice, and dismantle inequity pave the way for more inclusive communities. Leadership through service becomes timeless when it bridges generational divides. Elders mentoring youth, and youth honoring the wisdom of experience, foster continuity and connection across time.

Service demands vision. It requires the ability to see what is not yet visible—potential in people, solutions in problems, and hope in hardship. Philanthropy plays a critical role in service legacies. Individuals and families who establish scholarships, foundations, or endowments contribute to generational uplift and systemic change. Legacy is not built in isolation.

It thrives in partnership. Collaborating with others—across sectors, backgrounds, and beliefs—ensures that service efforts are sustainable and far-reaching. A service-minded leader asks, 'What can I do for others?' and then listens deeply before acting. This posture of humility and inquiry builds trust and effectiveness. Public servants who center their work in service rather than politics create legacies rooted in unity and progress.

Their decisions prioritize people over power and humanity over bureaucracy. Sometimes the most meaningful service is showing up in crisis—offering shelter in a storm, support in loss, or simply a steady presence in chaos. These moments define us. A true legacy requires succession. Investing in emerging leaders, documenting lessons learned, and creating leadership pipelines ensure that service outlives the individual.

Ultimately, to serve is to love in action. When we lead with our hearts, fueled by conviction and compassion, we leave behind more than deeds—we leave behind inspiration, transformation, and enduring hope. To create a legacy through service is to be a bridge between challenges and solutions. The most impactful leaders don't just identify problems—they mobilize people and resources to solve them collaboratively. Service-oriented leaders develop systems that outlast their direct involvement.

They are architects of sustainable change, designing programs and practices that continue to thrive under new leadership. In the realm of education, service can manifest in curriculum reform that reflects diverse experiences, or in developing programs that ensure equity in access and support for all learners. Legacy is shaped not just by what we give, but how we give. Service offered with humility, cultural sensitivity, and deep respect has a longer-lasting and more positive impact. The most enduring legacies are marked by alignment—when one's words, values, and actions consistently reflect a commitment to others.

This congruence cultivates trust and inspires others to do the same. Acts of service, when consistently modeled by those in leadership, influence workplace and community culture. Over time, what begins as isolated examples of kindness become institutionalized norms of care. Corporate leaders who center service in their organizational culture find that success is not diminished by generosity—it is amplified. Employee engagement, customer loyalty, and innovation all flourish under service-first leadership.

To leave a legacy of service is to recognize that influence is a gift, not a given. It must be stewarded with integrity, accountability, and a deep sense of responsibility to those we serve. Leaders who prioritize service often find their own lives enriched. While they pour into others, they receive in return: perspective, gratitude, purpose, and connection to something greater than themselves. Service transcends boundaries.

It bridges gaps between rich and poor, young and old, urban and rural. When we serve, we affirm our shared humanity and participate in building a more just and unified world. The measure of a leader's legacy is not found in accolades or titles, but in the number of lives uplifted through their service. The seeds sown in moments of generosity grow into forests of transformation. One of the clearest signs of a lasting service legacy is replication.

When others begin to mimic your model of impact, your service becomes a movement rather than a moment. For principals and educational leaders, legacy is built in the quiet victories—when a struggling student finds their voice, when a discouraged teacher is reignited with purpose, or when a school culture becomes one of compassion and collaboration. In corporate spaces, leaders who champion service-oriented policies—such as paid volunteer time, community partnerships, and inclusive hiring—reshape the purpose of business to serve both profit and people. When public policy is guided by service, the result is governance that responds with empathy. Policies become not only more just, but more humane and equitable.

In times of societal upheaval, leaders with service legacies rise not with louder voices, but with calming presence. They become steady hands, reminding communities of shared values and collective strength. A true legacy honors those who came before while lighting the path for those who follow. This dual commitment ensures that service is rooted in wisdom and extended through innovation. To mentor is to multiply.

Leaders who mentor with the intention of equipping others to lead with service create cascading layers of influence that extend their legacy well beyond their direct reach. Civic engagement is a powerful tool of service. Voting, organizing, educating others, and holding institutions accountable are all acts that contribute to a healthier, more responsive society. The soul of service is sacrifice, but not the kind that leaves one depleted. It is the type of sacrifice that nourishes—a conscious exchange of comfort for purpose, of convenience for meaning.

A servant leader does not measure success by how far they rise, but by how many others they lift along the way. The height of a legacy is determined by the depth of its impact. Legacy through service is not a single act but a sustained commitment. It's a pattern of putting others first, of aligning time and resources with values that extend beyond the self. Faith-based leaders often anchor their legacies in a calling to serve others.

Their ministries, outreach programs, and spiritual leadership transform lives, not by preaching alone but through lived example. Communities thrive when citizens step into service—not waiting for permission, but acting from conviction. Local leaders, volunteers, and everyday advocates shape the character of neighborhoods and cities. Those who build service legacies understand that failure is part of the process. Mistakes become lessons, and setbacks become setups for greater impact when approached with humility and resilience.

A powerful way to extend a service legacy is through storytelling. When leaders share not only their successes but also their struggles, they invite others to believe in their own capacity to serve. Service intersects with innovation when we ask, 'How can we solve problems better for more people?' Innovators in health, technology, education, and sustainability are redefining service on a global scale. The language of legacy is universal, but its dialects are diverse. Whether spoken in boardrooms or schoolyards, in homes or halls of power, the message is the same: we are here to help each other.

When organizations embrace service as a core value, they move from transactional to transformational. Customers become partners, employees become advocates, and missions become movements. The ultimate reward for a life of service is not applause but alignment—the deep sense of peace and purpose that comes from living a life that mattered to others. True legacy is not etched in stone but in the hearts and habits of those touched by our service. It lives on in the way people treat each other after we're gone.

Some of the most impactful service legacies come from those who work quietly behind the scenes—feeding families, tutoring children, comforting the grieving. Their humility is the foundation of their influence. Leaders who are intentional about service empower others to serve. They train successors, delegate authority, and model behaviors that become standard practice within an organization or community. Alumni programs, mentorship networks, and community advisory boards are excellent tools to preserve service legacies and ensure that influence is passed on strategically rather than accidentally.

Legacy can also be formalized through storytelling mediums like books, podcasts, and public speaking. When leaders reflect openly, they multiply their reach and reinforce their values across generations. A service legacy does not require perfection—it requires consistency. The ongoing effort to show up for others, even when imperfect, earns trust and transforms lives. When leaders connect their service to systemic change, they move from charity to justice.

They not only meet immediate needs but also challenge and reform the structures that create those needs. Some legacies are born from pain. Survivors of injustice, tragedy, or hardship who choose to serve others from that experience transform personal trauma into communal healing. Effective service legacies balance urgency and patience. They respond quickly to crises while building systems and structures for long-term, sustainable impact.

Service through policy, innovation, or mentorship becomes a legacy when others begin to say, 'Because of them, I now serve too.' This ripple effect is the highest compliment a servant leader can receive. Creating a legacy through service also requires discernment—knowing when to act, when to listen, and when to step aside to let others lead. A lasting legacy is collaborative, not controlling. Leadership that values service fosters environments of inclusion. When individuals feel seen and heard, they are more likely to serve others in turn, creating a ripple of goodwill and impact.

The integration of service into one's daily routine—whether checking on a neighbor, mentoring a colleague, or offering a kind word—cements service as a lifestyle rather than a special event. Organizations that honor the legacies of service often implement institutional memory practices: awards, commemorations, named initiatives, and living archives that teach future generations. The ability to serve cross-generationally—connecting youth with elders and vice versa—strengthens community ties. It allows wisdom and innovation to flow in both directions. A service legacy thrives when leaders are vulnerable.

Sharing lessons learned from failures, moments of doubt, and seasons of struggle humanizes leaders and invites authentic connection. Educational institutions can embed service into their mission statements and pedagogy, producing graduates who understand that their skills are not only tools for advancement but instruments for change. Spiritual and cultural traditions across the world affirm the power of service. From sacred texts to oral histories, serving others has always been a pathway to fulfillment and purpose. Leaders who understand the spiritual dimensions of service often approach their work with reverence.

They see each act of kindness as sacred and each life impacted as a testament to their values. Service-based leadership is not defined by position but by posture. Anyone, regardless of role, can leave a legacy when they lead with compassion, conviction, and commitment to community. Legacy is reinforced through intentional succession planning. Leaders of impact take care not only to serve but to prepare others to carry the torch of service forward with clarity and courage.

True service legacies are built on relationships, not just results. People remember how they were treated, how they were inspired, and how they were supported more than any single achievement. To sustain a service legacy, leaders must continually renew their 'why.' Reflection, journaling, and personal retreats are tools that help realign daily actions with deeper purpose. Service becomes legacy when it bridges the gap between dreams and opportunities for others. It's the teacher who encourages a student to believe in college, the coach who inspires discipline, the neighbor who opens a door.

Technology can be leveraged to expand service legacies. From digital learning platforms to nonprofit fundraising apps, innovation helps amplify positive influence at scale. Every community has hidden heroes—those who serve without recognition or reward. Honoring them publicly can reinforce a culture where service is valued and modeled. Legacy requires resilience.

There will be days when your service feels unseen or your efforts seem to fall short. But consistency in showing up builds a track record that time will vindicate. Environmental stewardship is another form of service legacy. Leaders who advocate for sustainability leave the world better for future generations, preserving the planet as part of their influence. In service, every act—no matter how small—has ripple effects.

A smile, a word of encouragement, or a meal shared may seem simple but can shift the course of someone's life. The end goal of a service legacy is not fame or recognition, but transformation. When lives, systems, and communities are changed for the better, the legacy becomes self-sustaining. Legacy built through service often transcends titles and roles. The custodian who takes pride in a clean environment, the bus driver who greets each student warmly—these quiet acts of leadership leave lasting marks.

To leave a legacy of service, one must choose daily to lead with empathy. It's not about waiting for perfect conditions, but about seeing every interaction as an opportunity to serve with intention. Service that becomes legacy is rooted in the belief that everyone matters.

Leaders who operate from this core conviction build cultures where people thrive and give their best. Leaders who prioritize service naturally attract others who value contribution.

This creates a virtuous cycle in which communities uplift themselves through shared commitment and compassion. Faith in others is central to legacy building. By mentoring, coaching, and sponsoring future leaders, we not only serve them but ensure the continuity of values and impact. A powerful legacy is shaped not just by what you do, but by what you inspire others to do. Leaders who empower others magnify their influence beyond what they alone could ever achieve.

Service-driven leadership is not afraid to get uncomfortable. Tackling difficult issues, advocating for the marginalized, and challenging injustice are vital components of a meaningful legacy. Every act of service sends a message. The consistency of those messages—of dignity, compassion, accountability, and vision—crafts a narrative that becomes your enduring story. True legacy work is intergenerational.

It involves listening to the wisdom of elders while investing in the dreams of the youth, creating a bridge that connects history to hope. When leaders adopt a mindset of abundance rather than scarcity, they serve with open hands. This generosity fuels trust and collaboration, which are hallmarks of transformative legacy. Service legacies are cultivated over time through habits, not just highlights. The day-to-day consistency of doing what's right, even when no one is watching, becomes the scaffolding of long-term impact.

Stories passed down from one generation to another often center around service—about someone who helped in times of need or showed kindness in moments of hardship. These stories inspire others to continue the chain. The most enduring legacies are those that are systematized. Leaders who institutionalize service through policies, programming, and organizational culture ensure it lives beyond their tenure. Service can be scaled when leaders empower teams.

Instead of being the sole source of action, they delegate with purpose and train others to take initiative aligned with shared values.

Digital legacies now play a larger role in service. Blogs, video journals, and podcasts allow servant leaders to preserve and share their insights, ensuring their influence reaches wide and deep. The emotional labor of service is real. Leaders who commit to legacy through service must also prioritize self-care and emotional resilience to sustain themselves for the journey ahead.

Service requires imagination. Leaders with lasting legacies dare to see a different future and then help others envision and work toward that possibility through action and hope. A hallmark of a legacy rooted in service is inclusion. Those who serve well seek out diverse voices and ensure that impact is not limited to a privileged few but benefits the broadest possible community. A single seed of service can grow into a forest of change.

Leaders who consistently model empathy, action, and courage create environments where service multiplies and regenerates. The final measure of a service legacy is not found in applause but in transformation. It is measured in lives uplifted, communities healed, and futures made brighter by someone's unwavering decision to serve. Legacy through service often blossoms in the quiet moments—the consistent follow-ups, the handwritten notes, the hours spent mentoring one individual. These seemingly small acts anchor a greater legacy.

Many leaders believe their legacy will be the work they complete, but in truth, it is the people they develop. Investing in others ensures that your influence carries forward through capable, compassionate hands. Communities evolve when leaders sow the seeds of service in young minds. Engaging youth in volunteerism, civic responsibility, and leadership development ensures the next generation continues the mission. A legacy of service is not about being needed forever; it's about making yourself unnecessary by building others up to lead.

The truest form of influence is when those you've helped no longer require your help. Recognition should not be the goal of service, but when used appropriately, it can validate and reinforce behaviors that strengthen collective purpose. Celebrating service inspires a culture that sustains it. Great service legacies often begin with a single cause that resonates deeply. Whether it's education, food security, justice, or mental health, aligning your passion with a problem empowers purpose.

Many service leaders are forged in adversity. Their empathy is born from struggle, making their legacy even more meaningful. These stories become powerful motivators for those facing similar challenges. Collaboration multiplies impact.

Leaders who foster partnerships with nonprofits, government, and community stakeholders expand their reach and deepen their footprint. Ethical clarity is vital for service-based legacies. When integrity guides decision-making, the trust built with communities becomes the foundation upon which lasting change is constructed. Ultimately, a service legacy lives in the lives you've touched, the voices you've uplifted, and the bridges you've built. It's not about having all the answers, but about showing up with a heart willing to help.

Creating a legacy of service often means resisting the urge to prioritize short-term gains over long-term contributions. Visionary leaders stay committed to the process, even when progress is slow or recognition is minimal. Service is not seasonal; it is a lifestyle. Those whose legacy is rooted in service approach each day with the intent to give—whether through time, resources, or simply kindness and encouragement. The ripple effects of service cannot be overstated.

One act of service can shift the trajectory of a family, a classroom, or a community, sparking a cycle of generosity and leadership that carries forward. A vital part of building a service legacy is understanding the needs of those being served. Leaders who listen deeply, ask meaningful questions, and tailor solutions build trust and lasting relevance. Legacy is strengthened by visibility. When leaders make their service efforts transparent and inclusive, they invite others to join, contribute, and carry on the mission beyond their personal reach.

To leave a lasting mark, servant leaders must also be students. Humility and a willingness to continue learning—especially from those they serve—ensure that their work remains responsive and relevant.

A leader's presence during a crisis can define their service legacy. Those who show up with calm, clarity, and compassion in difficult times earn respect that resonates far beyond their tenure. Service legacies are made stronger when they evolve.

As new challenges arise, enduring leaders adjust their methods without losing their core values, demonstrating adaptability and resilience. Mentorship is one of the most powerful tools of service-based leadership. By pouring into others, leaders duplicate their values and vision across generations, building an exponential impact. Legacy isn't about perfection—it's about persistence. Those remembered most fondly are not those who never failed, but those who showed up consistently, with integrity and a heart for others.

The act of service becomes transformative when it's aligned with a deeper mission. Leaders who root their efforts in purpose are more likely to inspire enduring change and loyal followership. When service is embedded in a leader's identity, every decision becomes an opportunity to uplift others. It's not just about leading projects—it's about cultivating people. Legacies are built by being present in the moment.

Leaders who listen attentively, respond compassionately, and engage authentically with others leave imprints that cannot be erased. Leaders often underestimate the power of reflection in sustaining service. Taking time to revisit motivations, evaluate impact, and learn from experiences ensures their legacy is intentional and evolving. It's not enough to serve in times of convenience. The strongest service legacies are forged in the discomfort of sacrifice—when leaders give despite challenges, setbacks, or fatigue.

Empowering others to serve multiplies influence. By creating systems that train and release other leaders, one person's service legacy becomes a community-wide movement. Courage is a silent partner in service. Leaders who stand for justice, speak on behalf of the marginalized, or resist apathy create legacies that challenge and transform the status quo. A service legacy can be sustained through documentation—writing books, delivering speeches, and mentoring successors.

These records extend a leader's reach beyond their lifetime. The mark of a truly impactful legacy is that it outlasts the leader. When the values, practices, and relationships nurtured during their time remain active after they're gone, their service continues to speak. Every generation has a choice—to consume or to contribute. Leaders who choose service sow the seeds of a better tomorrow, one action, one relationship, and one vision at a time.

Service that leaves a legacy is intentional. Leaders don't stumble into lasting influence—they plan for it, strategize it, and remain faithful to the cause, even when results take time. Cultural shifts often begin with a single servant leader. By modeling humility, respect, and commitment, one individual can catalyze transformation across an entire organization or community. Legacy is not built in the peaks of recognition but in the valleys of unseen effort.

It's in the extra hour, the kind correction, the consistent check-in that true impact is formed. Those who lead through service often prioritize sustainability. They develop others, establish systems, and teach replicable models so that their work doesn't end with them. A lasting legacy requires resilience. The road of service is often marked by setbacks and criticism, yet servant leaders press on, guided by their values rather than public opinion.

Legacy grows when leaders create space for others to lead. Encouraging new voices, inviting fresh ideas, and stepping aside at the right time ensure that service remains dynamic and relevant. True servant leaders build bridges across differences. They recognize that diversity strengthens impact, and they foster inclusive environments where all contributions are valued. A service-driven legacy can often be measured not just in programs launched but in people healed—those who found hope, purpose, or healing through another's dedication to serve.

Leaders who view service as sacred see every interaction as meaningful. Whether addressing a crowd or speaking to one, they operate with the same level of intentionality and care. In the final measure, legacy is love in action. It's the steady, selfless investment into others, carried out with conviction and joy, that defines a life well led and a legacy well earned. The enduring power of a service legacy lies in how it inspires future generations.

When young leaders witness authenticity, perseverance, and compassion in action, they inherit a model worth emulating. To secure a lasting legacy, leaders must periodically pass the torch. Knowing when to mentor rather than manage, guide rather than govern, is the hallmark of a mature, service-minded leader. The legacy of service flourishes when it is not bound to a single location or platform. Whether in classrooms, boardrooms, or neighborhoods, great leaders carry their mission wherever they go.

At its core, legacy is less about what a leader accomplishes and more about what they awaken in others. A well-lived life of service kindles courage, creativity, and compassion in countless hearts. As a chapter closes on any leadership journey, what endures is not the applause or the accolades, but the people changed, the lives elevated, and the culture transformed through faithful service. True legacy is never self-serving. It is built in the countless moments when a leader chooses people over pride, impact over image, and purpose over prestige.

As the sun sets on any chapter of leadership, those who served with consistency and heart will be remembered not for titles held, but for lives touched. To lead through service is to live a life of continuous giving—an echo of generosity that outlasts time, outshines recognition, and outlives the leader.

Chapter 13: A Call to Positive Action

Positive influence is not just a philosophy; it is a mandate for meaningful living. In a world where negativity often dominates headlines and despair weighs heavily on communities, there is a pressing need for individuals to step forward as beacons of hope, courage, and purposeful action.

A call to positive action begins with self-awareness. It is in understanding our values, strengths, and passions that we discover how we can uniquely contribute to the greater good. Every individual has the capacity to lead by example and become a source of inspiration to those around them. Action rooted in positivity does not wait for ideal conditions. It is proactive, intentional, and relentless in its pursuit of transformation.

Leaders who answer this call do not shrink in the face of adversity—they rise, knowing that each step forward matters. True positive action creates ripples. One act of kindness, one courageous stand, or one consistent effort can ignite a movement. It is not the magnitude of the action that counts, but the authenticity and commitment behind it. The call to action is not reserved for titles or roles.

Whether you are a teacher, a coach, a parent, a student, or a business owner, your influence is profound when you choose to act with integrity, empathy, and resilience. Positive action is often quiet, unnoticed, and deeply personal. It happens in the unseen moments when someone chooses patience over frustration, grace over judgment, and generosity over self-interest. These choices may seem small, but over time, they shape communities, cultures, and character. Responding to the call of positive influence means standing firm in your convictions.

It means choosing ethical paths even when shortcuts tempt you. It's about advocating for what is right, not what is easy or popular. Leaders who answer this call consistently find ways to uplift others. They praise effort, cultivate belief, and invest time in mentoring. They do not hoard knowledge or power but see their success as an opportunity to empower the next generation.

At the heart of every action is intention. To lead positively, one must be intentional about the impact they wish to leave. This requires reflection, humility, and a willingness to evolve. It also demands courage to confront complacency in ourselves and our environments. Positive action builds momentum.

As one person leads with compassion, others are inspired to do the same. Workplaces become more collaborative, schools become more supportive, and neighborhoods become more connected. The ripple effect is real—and it starts with one choice. Taking positive action also requires vision—an ability to see potential where others see problems. Leaders who possess this mindset are not deterred by limitations; they are energized by possibilities.

They ask, 'What could be?' and then work tirelessly to make it real. Courage is a cornerstone of positive influence. It takes courage to lead with hope in the face of skepticism, to model integrity when shortcuts are common, and to choose optimism when fear dominates the narrative. True influence does not demand attention; it earns respect. It doesn't shout to be heard; it listens to understand.

The most powerful actions are often those done quietly—acts of service, empathy, forgiveness, and love that affirm the humanity of others. Accountability is another hallmark of positive leadership. Those who act with intention must also be willing to own their impact. When mistakes are made, they take responsibility, learn, and grow. This level of humility builds trust and deepens influence.

To sustain positive action over time, one must also nurture themselves. Leaders often give so much to others that they neglect their own renewal. Rest, reflection, and reconnection to purpose are essential to ensure that action flows from a place of strength, not exhaustion. The call to positive action is also an invitation to collaborate. No leader makes lasting change alone.

It is through strategic partnerships, collective dreaming, and shared responsibility that movements are born and sustained. Service-driven leadership thrives when people see themselves as stewards of possibility. This mindset moves beyond transactional roles and embraces transformational purpose. It reframes success from individual gain to collective impact. In every generation, there are voices who rise to answer the call—voices that echo beyond their time, because their words were matched by action.

These are not just leaders by title but visionaries by choice. Their influence lingers because they dared to care deeply and act boldly. We live in an era that desperately needs such voices. Whether in classrooms, boardrooms, city halls, or community centers, we need leaders willing to act with hope and humility. Positive action has never been more urgent—or more powerful.

Let us not underestimate the significance of ordinary efforts. Smiling at a stranger, mentoring a young person, choosing fairness in a difficult conversation—these are acts of radical influence. When done consistently, they shift cultures and elevate human dignity. To act positively is to become an architect of legacy. Every decision we make constructs the framework of our influence.

When our actions are guided by compassion and consistency, we build something that will stand the test of time. Legacy is not found in accolades but in the lives touched. A leader's worth is measured by the impact they make on others' growth, their ability to inspire belief in potential, and their unwavering presence in moments of uncertainty. Positive action requires vision and alignment. When your internal values are synchronized with your external behaviors, your leadership becomes magnetic.

People are drawn to authenticity and consistency more than charisma or authority. To lead with impact is to ask, 'What will they remember about how I made them feel?' Emotional resonance is the soul of influence. It's not just about solving problems—it's about restoring faith, igniting purpose, and nurturing growth. Empowering others is one of the most selfless forms of positive action. When we teach others to lead, we multiply our impact.

True leaders build bridges for others to cross, rather than walls to elevate themselves. In moments of adversity, positive action becomes a defiant act of hope. When systems fail, when doubt looms, when injustice threatens, it is the consistent choice to believe in change that drives transformation. Leaders must be the calm in chaos and the spark in stillness. Cultural shifts do not occur through grand gestures alone.

They begin with a thousand quiet revolutions—staff members who advocate for equity, students who step up to lead with empathy, parents who model responsibility. These everyday champions form the backbone of societal progress. The mindset of a servant leader centers on 'we' instead of 'me.' It recognizes that individual achievement pales in comparison to collective success. Such leaders relinquish ego to uplift their teams, knowing that mutual respect yields the greatest results. Positive influence requires vigilance.

It is not enough to start strong—consistency must follow. The habits we build in private determine the integrity we show in public. Leaders must be disciplined stewards of their own character, lest their impact become accidental rather than intentional. Storytelling is a powerful tool for fostering positive action. When we share our struggles, our progress, and our purpose, we connect on a human level.

These stories become roadmaps for others, giving them courage to persevere and tools to navigate their own challenges. Positive action must also be intersectional—it must account for the diverse experiences, challenges, and strengths within a community. Leaders must intentionally listen to voices that are often unheard and amplify them in rooms where decisions are made. Sometimes, the most radical act of leadership is simply showing up—showing up with compassion when others retreat in discomfort, showing up with resolve when the path is unclear, and showing up for others even when applause is absent. Every leader is a mirror reflecting what is possible.

If we reflect doubt, fear, or indifference, we replicate these qualities in our teams. But if we embody courage, humility, and grace, we plant those same seeds in others—seeds that will grow long after we're gone. It is important to celebrate progress. Too often, we overlook milestones because we are chasing a finish line that keeps moving. Recognizing growth keeps morale high and reminds everyone involved that their efforts matter and their work is seen.

To act positively is to love relentlessly—not in the romantic sense, but in the unconditional commitment to the good of others. This love is expressed through fairness, forgiveness, truth-telling, and a refusal to give up on people, even when it's inconvenient. Resilience is a crucial companion to positive action. Without resilience, intentions fade when faced with resistance. But with resilience, even the most challenging setbacks become setups for comebacks, and leaders emerge stronger, clearer, and more compassionate.

The ripple effect of one bold choice can alter the trajectory of countless lives. A principal who reimagines discipline as restoration rather than punishment, a manager who invests in mentorship instead of micromanagement—these decisions shift culture. Leaders must also challenge their own comfort zones. Growth rarely happens in convenience. True leadership means risking criticism, confronting injustice, and standing up for values even when doing so costs us popularity or approval.

When we talk about positive action, we cannot forget the importance of clarity. A vision not clearly communicated is a vision that dies in silence. Leaders must articulate the 'why' behind every initiative and connect it to purpose that others can internalize. It is easy to underestimate how many people are waiting for someone to believe in them. Your simple words of encouragement, your willingness to extend grace, and your example of perseverance can be the spark that ignites someone else's breakthrough.

A call to positive action is a call to presence. Leaders must be present emotionally, intellectually, and physically. When we are truly present, we notice what others miss. We anticipate needs, we listen actively, and we respond with empathy and insight. Too many communities suffer from leadership absenteeism—not because roles are vacant, but because hearts are disengaged.

The most impactful leaders re-engage by restoring trust, rebuilding credibility, and re-centering purpose. Small, consistent steps often matter more than major one-time efforts. The leader who checks in regularly, who follows through on promises, who remembers names and personal stories—this leader builds trust brick by brick. Positive action is courageous because it often goes against the grain. It challenges toxic norms, outdated traditions, and complacent thinking.

To be a force for good is to be willing to be misunderstood, especially when you lead with integrity in a world accustomed to shortcuts. Mentorship is an expression of long-term positive action. It extends our reach beyond the present moment, ensuring that what we've learned is passed on, refined, and expanded by the next generation. In mentorship, legacy becomes living. Positive action is not always loud.

It often works quietly in the background—an encouraging email, a moment of active listening, a resource shared with no expectation of recognition. The power lies in the consistency of intention and impact. Community transformation is sustained by leaders who embrace responsibility as a privilege, not a burden. These leaders don't wait for external validation to do what is right. Their internal compass guides them toward service, compassion, and equity.

In environments where hope is fragile, positive leaders become architects of belief. They build bridges between despair and possibility, between past trauma and future opportunity. Through vision and vulnerability, they help others rewrite their narratives. The ripple of positive action can only extend as far as the leader's integrity allows. This is why self-work is essential.

Leaders must do the hard internal labor—healing their own wounds, confronting bias, and anchoring their choices in values, not ego. We must redefine success as significance. Not just what we achieve, but who we elevate along the way. Not only the goals we accomplish, but the grace with which we lead others toward their own victories. When we operate from a place of purpose, every action becomes an opportunity to inspire.

Purpose fuels direction, and direction sharpens influence. Leaders who live out their purpose ignite it in others, cultivating a culture where positivity multiplies. Positive action must also be intersectional. It considers the unique barriers people face based on race, gender, ability, and socioeconomic background. True leadership sees difference as strength and builds structures where everyone has equitable access to opportunity.

The courage to act positively is often born in adversity. Those who have faced trials and still choose to lead with empathy, those who've experienced loss and still sow hope—these are the leaders who transform systems from the inside out. As we lead with action, we must also lead with imagination. What could our communities look like if healing, innovation, and opportunity were at the center of every decision? Imaginative leaders shift paradigms and move people beyond survival into possibility.

Every generation needs torchbearers—those who will not only carry forward the light of positive influence but will also teach others how to spark their own flames. Our charge is not simply to act, but to multiply impact through shared ownership of progress. Positive action doesn't wait for permission. It is proactive, not reactive. Great leaders see the cracks in the system and step forward with solutions, even when no one else is watching.

They act not out of obligation but out of conviction. The true measure of influence lies not in how many people follow you, but in how many are inspired to lead after you. Positive leadership is inherently replicable—it cultivates leaders, not followers. In the face of apathy, positive action is a form of protest. It resists complacency, refuses to normalize injustice, and insists on progress.

A committed leader wakes up each day asking, 'What good can I do today?' and pursues the answer relentlessly. When we build organizations and communities rooted in love and accountability, we create environments where everyone has the chance to thrive. These spaces do not happen by accident—they are the result of intentional, sustained leadership choices. The invitation to act positively is open to everyone. It does not require a title or platform.

It requires awareness, courage, and a belief that even small actions can create significant impact when done consistently and authentically. Positive action invites us to consider legacy in motion. Not just what we leave behind, but what we build while we are here. Every decision becomes a brick in the foundation of someone else's opportunity. Those who lead from a place of purpose are not confined by fear.

They understand that growth often requires disruption, and they are willing to challenge comfort zones for the sake of progress. The fabric of a thriving society is sewn together by countless acts of courage, grace, and service. Leaders who consistently contribute these threads ensure that the collective future is one of strength and beauty. Positive leadership includes the discipline of listening—deep, empathetic listening that hears not only the words but the needs behind them. Leaders who truly listen unlock pathways to meaningful change.

To be a force for good, we must learn to balance urgency with sustainability. Positive impact isn't about fast fixes; it's about systems and mindsets that endure beyond the moment, shaping generations to come. Community transformation does not require perfection; it requires presence. Leaders who show up consistently—even in uncertainty—create trust, which is the currency of influence. Positive action demands that we move from intention to execution.

A dream without action is just a wish. Visionary leaders are those who pair their passion with persistence and create a trail of measurable outcomes. In today's world, saturated with noise and distraction, clarity of values becomes revolutionary. Leaders who remain anchored in integrity cut through confusion and draw others to a higher standard. Action without empathy is hollow.

Effective leadership must be human-centered. When we root our strategies in compassion, we create environments where others not only perform, but belong. We must also lead intergenerationally—mentoring upward and downward. Wisdom is not exclusive to age or title. When we create a reciprocal exchange of knowledge, we form communities where leadership is both taught and caught.

We cannot afford to wait for the world to change before we decide to act. Instead, we must be the catalyst for the change we wish to see, stepping boldly into challenges and pushing against the tide of stagnation. Every step of positive influence leaves a footprint in the lives of others. Whether through mentorship, advocacy, or innovation, leaders create ripples that often outlive their immediate visibility. One of the greatest calls to action is recognizing the power of the ordinary.

It's not always in grand gestures, but in the consistency of daily discipline, humility, and service that true leadership flourishes. It's not enough to point out what's wrong with the world—we must roll up our sleeves and help build what's right. Leaders who engage this way do more than inspire; they mobilize. Actionable hope is the engine of sustainable progress. Leaders who choose to infuse their work with hope, not naivety, become bridges between vision and execution.

They believe in what's possible and push forward even when others doubt. Leadership is not reserved for those in high offices or formal roles. It belongs to the everyday person who dares to live with purpose and conviction. The parent, teacher, coach, and community volunteer all wield the power of influence. A call to positive action also includes the courage to unlearn.

We must be willing to release mindsets, habits, and systems that no longer serve our collective growth and be open to more inclusive and effective ways of moving forward. We are accountable not only for what we say and do, but for the culture we allow to persist in our presence. Leaders who understand this responsibility stand guard over the environments they influence. Service-driven leadership shifts the spotlight from self to others. It redefines success through the lens of significance—how many lives are touched, how many voices are lifted, and how many barriers are broken.

In the face of adversity, positive leaders do not retreat. They rise. They find strength in their vision and resilience in their community, choosing to lead from a place of restoration rather than reaction. Positive influence multiplies when it is shared. Leaders who mentor others create legacy, not just impact.

They empower new voices and equip emerging leaders with the courage to act. Vision must always lead to movement. The best ideas, no matter how bold, have no value if they remain unacted upon. The bridge between inspiration and transformation is consistent application. A call to action also demands deep listening.

To lead effectively, we must first hear the heartbeats of those we serve. Real solutions come from understanding real needs, not assumptions. The measure of leadership is not in how well we are praised in public, but in how responsibly we act when no one is watching. Quiet decisions often shape the loudest outcomes. We must also recognize that change is rarely convenient.

It requires us to disturb the comfortable, challenge the status quo, and be willing to endure discomfort in the pursuit of justice and equity. There is a fierce urgency in our time to lead with compassion and conviction. Communities are calling for healing, institutions are crying for reform, and individuals are yearning for leaders who will act with integrity. A call to positive action requires emotional intelligence. Leaders must not only understand systems but also empathize with people.

It is this ability to connect humanely that amplifies influence and ensures sustainable outcomes. Accountability must accompany action. Vision without responsibility can become vanity. When leaders hold themselves to a standard of service and transparency, they create trust and inspire loyalty. We cannot be paralyzed by the fear of imperfection.

Action taken in good faith, with a willingness to learn and grow, can do far more good than waiting for flawless conditions that never arrive. When leaders show up authentically—unafraid to speak truth, admit faults, and remain teachable—they create space for others to do the same. Vulnerability becomes a strength, not a weakness. The heart of every meaningful movement is a group of people willing to act when others hesitate. They become the catalysts of change not because they have all the answers, but because they refuse to stay silent in the face of need.

Too often, people underestimate the value of small, consistent action. A single word of encouragement, a kind gesture, or a moment of support can change the course of someone's life. Positive action is contagious. When one person chooses to lead with integrity, others are inspired to do the same. Momentum builds, and what once felt impossible becomes a shared mission of hope.

It is born from the intersections of collaboration, sacrifice, and courage. Those who leave a lasting mark are those who consistently place service above self. The most enduring leaders are those who understand that change is not a sprint, but a relay. Their goal is not just to finish strong, but to hand the baton of progress to others who will continue the race with excellence.

The call to positive action is not reserved for those with titles or authority—it is an open invitation to every individual who chooses to care. Influence begins the moment we decide to be intentional with our presence. In every sphere—education, business, community service, and family life—there are moments that ask us to stand up, speak out, and step in. These moments may not come with applause, but they shape our character and our legacy. It is easy to critique systems and wait for others to fix them.

It is harder, and far more noble, to roll up our sleeves and do the hard work of building something better. Every challenge we face presents an opportunity to model courage. When leaders meet adversity with grace and resolve, they model to others that fear does not have the final word. A life of positive action is a life marked by purpose. It aligns our choices with our values, our strengths with our service, and our leadership with our legacy.

Answering the call to positive action means choosing contribution over comfort. It requires stepping outside of routines to embrace growth, advocacy, and the sometimes-uncomfortable pursuit of justice. Change is rarely convenient. Those who wait for the perfect moment to act are often left behind. Leaders recognize that progress is forged in the trenches of discomfort and determination.

The most powerful influence is lived, not proclaimed. People are inspired by what we do far more than by what we say. Our actions set the tone for the culture we create around us. Everyday leadership emerges in classrooms, boardrooms, churches, and community centers. It flourishes when ordinary people make extraordinary commitments to kindness, fairness, and the common good.

The world doesn't need more spectators. It needs builders, mentors, encouragers, and innovators—those willing to put vision into motion and lift others as they climb. To lead with positive influence is to be deeply invested in outcomes that benefit others, not just ourselves. It is to seek justice, promote equity, and extend empathy even when the path forward is unclear. Social change does not always begin in the spotlight.

Many movements are sparked by quiet convictions—by individuals who see a need and respond with courage and compassion. Action rooted in values creates sustainable transformation. When our initiatives are grounded in integrity and authenticity, they have the power to resonate across generations. One of the most radical acts in today's world is hope. Hope that change is possible, hope that our collective voice matters, and hope that the next generation will inherit something better than we found.

We rise by lifting others. Positive action should always have a ripple effect, encouraging others to recognize their own capacity to make a difference and step into their own leadership journey. A culture of positive action must be cultivated intentionally within every community. It starts with conversations, grows through collaboration, and endures through commitment. Let us not underestimate the influence of a single act of encouragement, mentorship, or advocacy.

Often, it is the smallest gestures that plant the seeds of significant change. When we model servant leadership, we challenge the narrative that success is about power or position. We demonstrate that true greatness is rooted in humility and generosity. As we navigate a complex and often divided world, choosing to be a source of unity, dignity, and purpose is a radical form of leadership. It signals that love still has the power to transform.

To sustain positive action, leaders must prioritize reflection, rest, and renewal. Replenished leaders lead better, influence deeper, and endure longer in their impact. Positive action is fueled by a deep understanding that our presence can shift atmospheres. When we walk into rooms with a commitment to uplift, encourage, and empower, transformation begins. Being a change agent often means being misunderstood.

Leaders committed to positive action must develop the emotional resilience to stay rooted in purpose, even in the face of resistance. Every community has latent brilliance—people with potential waiting to be recognized and nurtured. Positive leaders are intentional about uncovering, cultivating, and celebrating that brilliance. We are each called to leave footprints of hope. Whether through education, entrepreneurship, advocacy, or service, our actions can pave a path of progress for those who follow us.

The ultimate measure of leadership is not what we accumulate, but what we activate in others. A legacy of positive influence is built through consistent, courageous, and compassionate action. True progress is not measured by how far we climb alone, but by how many we lift as we ascend. Positive leaders view every achievement as an opportunity to elevate others. The call to positive action is both personal and collective.

Each individual's efforts matter, but lasting transformation occurs when communities unite around shared values and purpose. Change begins with awareness but is sustained through action. It is not enough to know what must be done—we must commit to doing it, consistently and courageously. Positive influence is an echo—it reverberates through the lives we touch, long after our direct presence fades. This is the essence of legacy.

The next generation is watching how we lead, serve, and speak. Our daily choices model for them what leadership looks like and set a precedent for the future they will shape. Positive action is not about perfection—it is about persistence. It is the daily decision to show up, speak up, and serve with intention and integrity. Movements of change often begin with a whisper—a single voice daring to question the norm.

When that voice is joined by others, it becomes a roar that cannot be ignored. Leaders who prioritize empathy alongside strategy build movements, not just moments. Their influence lives beyond organizational charts and becomes embedded in culture. In every space we enter, we carry the potential to leave it better than we found it. This is the responsibility and privilege of being a positive influence.

Let us respond to the call of our times with courage. Let us lead with vision. Let us act with compassion. And above all, let us be relentless in our pursuit of a better future for all. We are each a ripple in a larger wave of progress.

The question we must ask ourselves daily is: what direction is my ripple flowing? Toward unity, justice, and growth—or away from it? A call to positive action demands not just our hands, but our hearts. It is a full-body, full-mind, full-soul commitment to lead lives that reflect the values we speak of. As educators, leaders, and community builders, we must ensure that the environments we create are rooted in belonging and empowerment.

Everyone should have the opportunity to contribute their voice. To act positively is to reject complacency. It is to see the cracks in the system and resolve not only to patch them—but to build something new, stronger, and more equitable. The time for impact is now. We cannot delay purpose, postpone progress, or procrastinate in compassion.

The world is waiting for our contribution. Let us answer the call—boldly, bravely, and with unwavering hope. Every generation inherits not just the world we leave behind, but the mindset we model. When we take positive action, we are investing in the collective consciousness of the future. Service, kindness, and courage are not outdated concepts—they are the blueprint for what the future demands.

Now is the time to normalize integrity and reimagine influence. A positive future is not promised; it must be pursued. With deliberate steps and faithful hearts, we must walk toward justice, education, opportunity, and healing. This is your moment. Whether you lead in a classroom, a boardroom, or on your block, your influence is real, and your action is needed.

Answer the call. Let your legacy be one of light, not shadow. Let your voice be one that echoes hope. Let your action be a seed that blossoms in others for years to come. Positive action does not require perfection, only participation.

Every step forward, no matter how small, contributes to a movement greater than ourselves. When we empower others through our influence, we unlock a chain of inspiration that multiplies far beyond what we can measure. Hope, when paired with action, becomes transformation. In every community, school, or workplace, the change we seek begins with the choice to act with conviction and compassion. A legacy of positive influence is not written in accolades but in the lives uplifted, the systems challenged, and the hearts inspired.

Let this be the call that stirs your spirit—because the future is not a distant place. It is the impact we create, one courageous act at a time.

Final Summary and Closing Takeaway

As we draw this journey to a close, it is important to reflect on the themes that have guided us through each chapter of this book. From the first step of understanding the impact of positive influence to the final call to action, this manuscript has explored the intricate dynamics of motivation, leadership, resilience, empathy, growth, and legacy. Whether as educators, executives, parents, or community leaders, understanding motivation is crucial for unlocking potential—in ourselves and in others. By learning how to cultivate intrinsic drive and align it with purposeful goals, we lay the groundwork for sustained influence. We must remember that every moment presents a choice—to lead passively or to lead with purpose. Passive leadership waits for the conditions to be right; purposeful leadership creates the conditions. The latter reshapes reality through vision, effort, and a belief in better outcomes.

Leaders who create a legacy of impact do not do so by chance. They do it by cultivating discipline, nurturing hope, and consistently acting in alignment with their values. They influence systems by investing in people. They know that institutions are only as strong as the relationships within them. As we think about the future of leadership, it is clear that adaptability, compassion, and collaboration will define the most effective influencers.

These traits allow us to respond to the unpredictable, connect across boundaries, and solve problems with collective wisdom. Leadership is also about storytelling—the stories we tell ourselves and the ones we help others to write. Every person you lead is crafting a narrative about who they are and what they can become. The best leaders help others believe in their worth and in the possibilities ahead. Sustainability in leadership means building frameworks that endure beyond your presence.

It means mentoring successors, institutionalizing equity, and documenting lessons so others can learn from your journey. True impact does not end when you step away; it echoes through systems and lives long after. Your influence is not limited to your job title or your resume. It lives in your daily decisions, your attitude in adversity, and your treatment of others. Influence is the byproduct of consistent intention and relentless authenticity.

To those who have walked this path of discovery through the pages of this manuscript, the charge is clear: Lead boldly. Influence positively. And remember, the world is waiting on your voice, your vision, and your unwavering values. Your time is now. Let your leadership be a light.

Let your life be an example. And let your legacy be built not on applause, but on the lives changed because you chose to lead with heart, head, and hands aligned. That is the power of positive influence for future impact. In times of uncertainty, leaders must be anchors. Your presence, steadiness, and commitment to values offer reassurance to those who follow you.

In being calm, clear, and courageous, you invite others to rise above fear and confusion into a space of clarity and strength. Transformation does not come through grand gestures alone. It is found in the follow-through, the quiet discipline of showing up and doing the work even when recognition is absent. True influence is developed in the trenches of consistency and the fires of responsibility. As we close this journey, let us reaffirm that leadership is not reserved for the few.

It belongs to the willing. You do not need permission to lead—you simply need to care enough to act, learn, and grow. Your story is valid. Your path is powerful. Your potential is limitless.

Carry this with you: leadership begins with belief. If you believe in your capacity to learn, your ability to serve, and your drive to make a difference, then you already possess the most essential tools of influence. The rest is refinement, commitment, and connection. And so, as the final chapter concludes, a new one begins—written by your hands, driven by your convictions, and marked by your service. May this book not be an end, but a launchpad. May you leave these pages ready to lead with renewed purpose and persistent passion.

Dr. Nigel L. Walker, born February 13, 1980, in Eufaula, AL, was raised by his mother, Jacqueline, alongside seven siblings in public housing. A lifelong learner, he earned his B.A., M.Ed., and Ed.S. in Education from LaGrange College, and his Doctorate from Columbus State University. A writer since youth, his published works include *STRIVE for Greatness: Motivation in Your Own Image and children's book, Cuddle Baby and Scuttle Bug: My Fraternal Twins*. Dr. Walker is an educator, consultant, author, speaker, and performer, currently serving as an elementary school principal. He is the owner of WILL Educational Services, LLC, and founder of the nonprofit Walker Success Academy, Inc. Dr. Walker is a member of Phi Beta Sigma Fraternity, Inc., and the hip-hop group Hypoetically Speaking. He resides in LaGrange, GA, with his wife, Irene, his daughters Emily and Claudia, and twin daughters Leah and Lydia.